ENTERTAINING IN THE COUNTRY
Love Where You Eat

ENTERTAINING IN THE COUNTRY
Love Where You Eat

FESTIVE TABLE SETTINGS, FAVORITE RECIPES, AND DESIGN INSPIRATION

JOAN OSOFSKY & ABBY ADAMS
Principal Photography by John Gruen

RIZZOLI
NEW YORK

New York Paris London Milan

TABLE OF CONTENTS

CAMILLE STYLES *entertaining* | INSPIRED GATHERINGS & EFFORTLESS STYLE

AMY CHAPLIN | at home in the whole food kitchen | CELEBRATING THE ART OF EATING WELL

INTRODUCTION

by Joan Osofsky

A drive up the Taconic Parkway over fifty years ago brought me to the small town of Pine Plains in New York's Dutchess County. It's a rural farming town with a population of just about two thousand. For a suburban New Jersey girl, I might as well have been in Kansas—but I was just two hours north of home. My eyes were wide open. There were rolling fields spotted with silos and Holstein cows, community square dances in the Grand Union parking lot, a country wedding where everyone in town was invited, and trash-and-treasure antiques shops brimful of vintage finds. It was the beginning of my lifelong love affair with country life: its beauty, charm, and authentic style. Life is taken down a notch here, slowed down and made simple.

In 1985, I launched my first Hammertown store in a historic barn in Pine Plains. I filled the store with antiques, gifts, kitchen gadgets, furniture, toys, cookbooks, and lots more—all the elements of modern country life. There are now three Hammertown Barn stores; in Rhinebeck, New York, and Great Barrington, Massachusetts, as well as the original in Pine Plains. Through them I've built a community of customers and friends who share my love of the country way of living.

Entertaining is at the core of the Hammertown style. Well before Martha Stewart, Lee Bailey's inspiring books were a strong influence, as was Mary Emmerling's *American Country: A Style and Source Book*, Julee Rosso and Sheila Lukins's *The Silver Palate Cookbook*, Ina Garten's *Barefoot Contessa* cookbooks, and Bunny Williams's fusion of food and style in *An Affair with a House*. If I think back, though, to one defining moment of inspiration, it was during my first year at Hammertown, and my first invitation to the Coach Farm annual fall party, at Miles and Lillian Cahn's goat farm in Gallatin, New York. The Cahns, former owners of Coach Leatherware and creators of the iconic Coach bag, were also recent converts to country living. Their former dairy farm, on a hill with gorgeous pastoral views, would soon become a state-of-the-art cheese-making facility.

Miles and Lillian were in a class of their own. Their style of entertaining was casual, organic, and welcoming, and reflected their love of life and each other. There were vintage linen tablecloths, marble slabs and wooden boards for serving cheese, English ironstone, French cutlery, baskets of flowers, scrubbed pine tables, art and artifacts.

Food has more meaning in farm country. At the Cahns's the fare was always elegant—Miles's signature dish was a massive choucroute garnie, dished up on white ironstone plates—and hearty, with plenty for everyone. Their home was the soul of their very being and you felt and tasted the love the minute you stepped inside. This feeling was what I wanted to communicate in my own entertaining, and in my work.

Entertaining in the Country is a testament to our friends, neighbors, and customers, and the lifestyle we have shared. Let this be an inspiration to take the beauty and produce of the countryside and bring it to your home—from your interiors to your table. Love Where You Eat!

POTLUCK SUPPER FOR FORTY

—Joan Osofsky

MENU

STARTERS
Rosey and Barry's
Chaseholm Cheeses

Leah's Green Beans with Peanut Dip

*Mary's Guacamole

*Abby's Brandade de Morue

MAINS
*Joan's Moroccan Brisket

Chris and Gayle's Baked Ham

Walter's Mom's Pasta Casserole

Jane and Jama's Vegetable Casserole

*Joan's Moussaka

SIDES
Moisha's Kale Salad

Jennifer and Nick's Sesame Noodles

*Rhonda's Mixed Salad

*Jack and Bob's Corn Pudding

*Jamie's Beet Salad

Chuck and Chuck's Corn Creole

Steve's Bread

DESSERTS
*Jeannette's Quesillo

*Barry's Apple Pie

Robin's Lemon Squares

Adrienne's Pear Tart

*Terry's Chocolate Hazelnut
Mousse Cake

Here in the country, when you invite people to dinner, they always ask: "What can I bring?" Recently, when some very dear friends of ours, Steven and Melissa Sorman, decided to relocate from the Hudson Valley to Minnesota, Abby and I decided to throw them a big good-bye party, a potluck. Potluck parties are great icebreakers.

In the invitation we encouraged our friends to let us know if they would *like* to bring something. (It would be terribly rude to demand that they do so.) For the next few weeks e-mails and phone calls flew back and forth as the menu evolved. We wanted to avoid duplicates—and to make sure that all the bases (starters, mains, desserts) were covered. I contributed two dishes, both recipes that have been in my repertory for years: a moussaka and a Moroccan-style beef brisket. Both are crowd-pleasers, can be made ahead of time, and are best served at room temperature. One friend brought a baked ham, always a good choice for a party: It's easy to serve and goes with everything. There were a number of hearty casseroles, several salads, and some stunning desserts. We made up cards for each dish with the name of the cook and the recipe title, and set them on place card holders. The cards made it easy to organize the party offerings. We put the starters near the bar, encouraging guests to mingle while we arranged the main-course platters on the long table in the kitchen. Desserts were set on a round table in the corner. The guests served themselves. Seating consisted of chairs around tables in three rooms, in addition to sofas. The party was a huge success. The variety of dishes made for a great grazing experience and the honorees—Steven and Melissa—had an unforgettable send-off.

With forty guests expected for the party, we set up tables—some small, like this one, some bigger—throughout the house. I like to arrange the napkins and flowers ahead of time. The branchlike wall sconces are a Hammertown favorite: I love their graceful organic shapes.

Potluck parties are great mixers; we had more than forty guests, some who didn't know anyone before that evening. By the end of the party everyone had made new friends.

Stage the bar at one end of the room (or in a separate room) from the hors d'oeuvres to keep the party flowing.

For a buffet dinner, look for recipes that can be made ahead of time and served at room temperature.

Make sure you've got extra serving dishes and utensils on hand. Anticipate needs, such as condiments, and lemons and parsley for garnish.

The kitchen at the big house at Hammertown Barn in Pine Plains: The antique hutch at far right serves as a pantry. Whenever I give a party, the guests inevitably cluster around the work island, which doubles as extra seating.

LEFT AND OPPOSITE: We set up the bar in a separate room from the kitchen. Ice, garnishes, and pretty cocktail napkins, along with opened bottles of wine and other beverages, are handy so that guests can help themselves. The basket beside the table is a useful receptacle for empty bottles and used napkins. The vegetable still life above the table is by photographer Lynn Karlin. ABOVE: Photographer Val Shaff took the soulful cow portrait that hangs on the kitchen wall. I love the different shapes and textures of these cutting boards and wooden bowl.

LEFT: The portrait on the wall is by an unknown Danish artist. OPPOSITE: This table, in the center of the main room, was set aside for the guests of honor. The Indian print tablecloths and napkins, with their pretty floral pattern, were a perfect match for my heirloom dishes. The combination made everyone think of spring, although it was still winter outside.

MELISSA
x

I've been collecting tole trays for many years. I love their shapes and rich hand-painted designs. I display them in various groupings; this arrangement makes a nice backdrop for the little votive candles. The fireplace surround is original to the house and dates to the early nineteenth century.

Mary's Guacamole

The multitalented Mary Murfitt (she's a musician, writer, and composer) brings this toothsome dip to parties all over the tristate area. She notes that guacamole should never be made more than one hour ahead of time.

Time: 15 minutes
Serves 6

2 ripe Hass avocados
1 to 2 garlic cloves, finely minced
1 tablespoon finely chopped fresh cilantro,
    plus a few extra sprigs for garnish
1 to 2 tablespoons medium-hot salsa
    (homemade or in a jar)
1 large lime
Kosher salt

1. Cut each avocado in half. Remove the pits (setting one aside) and scoop out the flesh with a teaspoon into a shallow bowl. Use a digging motion rather than scooping out in one big piece. The avocados will be easier to mash later.

2. Add the garlic, cilantro, and salsa to the avocados.

3. Cut the lime in half. Squeeze the juice from one of the halves into the bowl. Save the other half.

4. Mash the ingredients together in the bowl, using the back of a fork, until the mixture is as smooth or chunky as you like. Taste the guacamole before adding salt because some salsas are heavily salted. Add more garlic to taste.

5. Place the reserved avocado pit in the middle of the guacamole to keep it fresh before serving. Cover with plastic wrap, but do not refrigerate.

6. To serve: Remove and discard the avocado pit. Garnish with lime slices and a few cilantro sprigs.

Abby's Brandade de Morue

This classic hors d'oeuvre from Provence—salt cod blended with potatoes, garlic, and olive oil—is served warm with croutons or crackers.

Time: Allow 24 hours for soaking the cod, then 1 hour for preparation. Can be made several days ahead.
Serves 20 to 40

1 pound skinless salt cod
1 pound boiling potatoes, peeled and
    cut into large chunks
1¾ cups whole milk
8 garlic cloves
1 cup extra virgin olive oil, plus more for
    coating the baking dish
½ teaspoon freshly ground black pepper
¼ cup freshly grated Parmesan cheese
1 long baguette, sliced in ¼-inch rounds, lightly toasted,
    (or crackers) for serving

1. Rinse the salt cod in water. Drain and then put the cod in a bowl with water to cover. Refrigerate for 24 hours, changing the water every few hours.

2. Preheat the oven to 400°F.

3. Cook the potatoes in plenty of water until soft, about 30 minutes. Drain the water and let the potatoes cool. Set aside.

4. Drain the salt cod and cut into 2-inch pieces. Transfer to a saucepan and cover with 2 inches of water. Bring to a boil, simmer for 2 minutes, then drain the water and rinse the pan. Repeat—it's important to fully rinse off the excess salt. Return the salt cod to the pan, add the milk and garlic, and bring to a boil. Add the cooked potato chunks and stir together. Cool to room temperature, then transfer the mixture to a food processor. Mix until smooth, then slowly add the olive oil, processing until the oil is absorbed. Add the pepper.

5. Oil the bottom and sides of an 8-inch round baking dish and spoon in the salt cod mixture. Sprinkle the Parmesan on top and bake for 20 minutes, or until the top is brown and bubbly.

CLOCKWISE FROM TOP RIGHT: Abby's brandade; Steve's homemade country loaf; cheeses from Rosey and Barry's family dairy, Chaseholm, including Moonlight Chaource and Camembert.

ROSEY + BARRY CHEESE PLATE

BRANDADE Abby

4 bay leaves

½ teaspoon ground cinnamon

2 to 3 cups low-sodium beef broth

3 cups red wine

1 to 2 cups dried apricots, some sliced and
some left whole

1 cup whole dried prunes

1 cup canned pitted green olives, halved

½ cup Wondra flour (optional, for the gravy)

1. Preheat the oven to 350°F.

2. Using the tip of a sharp paring knife, make twelve evenly spaced small slits about 1 inch deep in the brisket. With your fingers, insert half of the garlic slices into the slits. Generously season the brisket with salt and pepper.

3. Heat a large pot on high heat for 2 to 3 minutes. Add 2 tablespoons of the olive oil and swirl it around, then add the meat and sear it for about 5 minutes on each side, or until nicely browned. Remove to a platter, and season again with salt and pepper.

4. Using paper towels, wipe out the casserole and return it to the stove. Turn the heat to medium and add the remaining 2 tablespoons olive oil. Add the onions and cook, stirring, until they are golden and soft, at least 10 minutes, then stir in the tomato paste, ½ cup water, bay leaves, and the remaining garlic slices. Return the meat to the pan, add the cinnamon, beef broth, and red wine. Make sure the liquid covers the meat. Add the apricots, prunes, and olives.

5. Bring the pot to a simmer on top of the stove, then transfer it to the oven. Turn the meat every 30 minutes. After about 2 hours, remove the meat from the oven and cut it into thick slices.

6. Put the sliced meat back in the pot, return the meat to the oven, and cook for another hour or so, until tender.

7. Allow the pot to come to room temperature. Refrigerate, covered, for at least 6 hours. Before serving, heat the oven to 350°F.

8. With a spoon, remove any extra fat. Return the pot to the oven and reheat until the sauce is bubbling, about 10 minutes. Serve hot or at room temperature.

9. To make optional gravy: Remove the sliced brisket and make a roux with Wondra flour or potato starch (if making at Passover).

Joan's Moroccan Brisket

This brisket, a true comfort dish, is an adaptation of a recipe a customer gave me a number of years ago. It's a family favorite, which I serve for Passover every year. The key to success: You need a great casserole or Dutch oven that holds the heat well. I have a Le Creuset, but any well-seasoned cast-iron pot will fit the bill.

Time: 3 hours. Make it the day before, and then reheat. Serves 10 to 12

One whole (about 5 pounds) beef brisket,
trimmed of most of the fat
7 garlic cloves, thinly sliced
Kosher salt and freshly ground black pepper
4 tablespoons good olive oil
3 large onions, thinly sliced
One 6-ounce can tomato paste

Joan's Moussaka

This favorite one-dish recipe is perfect for a crowd.

Time: 1 hour. Make a day ahead.
Serves 12

3 medium eggplants (about 3 pounds)
1 tablespoon kosher salt
3 tablespoons extra virgin olive oil, plus more for
    coating the parchment paper
3 onions, chopped
2 pounds ground lamb
One 6-ounce can tomato paste
2 cups red wine
$\frac{1}{2}$ cup fresh flat-leaf parsley, roughly chopped
$\frac{1}{4}$ teaspoon ground cinnamon
Freshly ground black pepper
6 tablespoons unsalted butter, plus more for
    coating the baking pan
6 tablespoons unbleached all-purpose flour
1 quart 2-percent milk, heated
4 large eggs, beaten
$\frac{1}{8}$ teaspoon ground nutmeg
2 cups ricotta cheese
1 cup panko bread crumbs
1 cup freshly grated Parmesan cheese

1. Preheat the oven to 400 F.

2. Precook the eggplant: Peel the eggplants and cut into $\frac{1}{2}$-inch slices. Spread the slices on paper towels and sprinkle all sides with the salt. Let sit for 30 minutes, then dry with paper towels. Line two baking sheets with parchment paper and coat lightly with olive oil. Arrange the eggplant slices in one layer, and drizzle 1 tablespoon of the olive oil on top. Bake for 10 minutes, then turn the slices over and bake for another 10 minutes, or until the eggplants are cooked through; they will be soft to the touch. Set aside.

3. Heat 2 tablespoons of the olive oil in a large saucepan. Add the onions and cook until translucent. Add the lamb and cook, breaking up the meat with a wooden spoon. When the meat is no longer pink, add the tomato paste, red wine, parsley, and cinnamon, and plenty of salt and pepper. Simmer over low heat until the sauce thickens. Set aside.

4. To make the béchamel sauce: Melt the butter in a small heavy-duty saucepan over low heat. Add the flour and cook for about 5 minutes, stirring. Slowly whisk in the warmed milk and cook until it begins to thicken, about 5 minutes. Remove from the heat and cool slightly. Combine the eggs, nutmeg, and ricotta in a small bowl, then stir the mixture into the roux. Set aside.

5. To assemble the moussaka: Butter an 11 by 16-inch baking dish and sprinkle the bottom with the panko. Arrange alternating layers of cooked eggplant slices and the lamb mixture, sprinkling each layer with Parmesan and the remaining panko. Pour the béchamel sauce over the top and sprinkle with more cheese and panko. Bake for 1 hour, or until the top is nicely browned. Serve warm or at room temperature.

Rhonda's Mixed Salad

Rhonda Cayea is my right- and left-hand help at Hammertown Barn. Her salads are a wonderful addition to any occasion.

Time: 5 minutes
Serves 12

2 heads hydroponic lettuce, washed and dried
2 cups mixed baby lettuces, washed and dried
Rhonda's Balsamic Salad Dressing (recipe follows)
½ cup dried cranberries
6 fresh strawberries, hulled and quartered
1 cup feta cheese, crumbled
1 cup candied walnuts

1. Tear the lettuces into bite-size pieces. Put them in a large salad bowl and dress with ½ cup balsamic vinaigrette. Toss to combine.

2. Add the cranberries, strawberries, feta cheese, and walnuts. Toss lightly, and serve.

RHONDA'S BALSAMIC SALAD DRESSING

Time: 5 minutes
Makes 1 cup

1 garlic clove, crushed
¼ cup balsamic vinegar
3 tablespoons honey
1 tablespoon Dijon mustard
½ teaspoon salt
½ teaspoon freshly ground black pepper
¾ cup extra virgin olive oil

In a small bowl, combine the garlic, balsamic vinegar, honey, mustard, salt, pepper, and olive oil, and whisk until thickened.

Note: Leftover salad dressing can be stored in the refrigerator, covered, for 2 weeks.

ABOVE AND OPPOSITE: Cards were made up ahead of time to identify the various dishes. The little metal cardholders came from Hammertown.

Jack and Bob's Corn Pudding

This satisfying casserole is simple to prepare: It's great on a buffet table or as a main course for a luncheon.

Time: 1 hour
Serves 8

6 ears fresh corn, preferably white and
    yellow mixed (or one 10-ounce package frozen corn
    kernels plus one 15-ounce can creamed corn)
1 cup whole milk
6 large eggs, beaten
1½ cups shredded mild Cheddar cheese
½ cup shredded Monterey Jack cheese
8 tablespoons (1 stick) unsalted butter, melted
1 bunch scallions, chopped
    (reserve green tops for garnish)
Kosher salt and freshly ground black pepper

1. Preheat the oven to 375°F.

2. To prepare the corn: Husk the ears and remove the corn silk. Scrape off the kernels with the milk (the liquid from the corncobs) into a large bowl.

3. Add the whole milk, eggs, Cheddar, Monterey Jack, butter, scallions, and salt and pepper to the bowl. Stir to combine.

4. Pour the mixture into a deep 8-inch cast-iron skillet (or any ovenproof baking dish), sprinkling on the scallion tops.

5. Bake for 40 minutes, or until the middle of the dish is just set. (If the top gets too brown while cooking, cover with a piece of aluminum foil.)

Note: The corn pudding is best served immediately. It can be reheated.

Jamie's Beet Salad

Jamie Purinton is a landscape architect and environ-mentalist. The beets in this delicious salad came from her large organic garden.

Time: 10 minutes
Serves 8

1 cup sliced pickled beets
¾ cup extra virgin olive oil
¼ cup white wine vinegar
Juice of ½ lemon
1 shallot, very finely chopped
Sea salt and freshly ground black pepper
4 cups fresh baby greens, such as arugula
    and spinach, washed and dried
½ cup soft goat cheese, in teaspoon-size pieces

1. Drain the beets and cut them into bite-size pieces.

2. To make the salad dressing: Combine the olive oil, vinegar, lemon juice, and shallot, and season with salt and pepper. Mix well, with a whisk, or in a blender or food processor.

3. To assemble the salad: Place the greens in a large bowl. Arrange the beet slices and pieces of goat cheese on top. Add the salad dressing just before serving, and toss lightly.

Note: The dressing will keep in the refrigerator, covered, for a week or more.

OPPOSITE: The buffet table, with all the main course dishes ready for the guests to serve themselves.

Jeannette's Quesillo

This Venezuelan flan is "as common as apple pie" in Jeannette Rollins's native Venezuela. The caramel coating makes for a lovely presentation.

Time: 10 minutes preparation, 45 minutes cooking, then 6 hours, refrigeration
Serves 6 to 8

3 tablespoons sugar
One 12-ounce can evaporated milk
One 14-ounce can sweetened condensed milk
3 large eggs
1 teaspoon pure vanilla extract
Pinch of salt

1. Preheat the oven to 350°F.

2. To make the caramel sauce: Heat the sugar in a small, heavy-bottomed saucepan over low heat. As the sugar begins to melt and turn brown, shake the pan so the sugar melts evenly.

3. Quickly spread the caramel on the sides and bottom of a 6-inch wide by 3-inch deep round ovenproof baking dish.

4. Combine the evaporated milk, condensed milk, eggs, vanilla, and salt in a blender and mix thoroughly. Pour the mixture into the caramel-coated baking dish, and bake for 45 minutes.

5. Allow the dish to cool to room temperature, then transfer it to the refrigerator, covered, for at least 6 hours.

6. To serve: Gently separate the custard from the baking dish with a knife and place on a cake plate.

Barry's Apple Pie

Barry Chase can always be counted on to bring a fabulous apple pie to a party. His secret ingredient—butter.

Time: 1 hour
Serves 8

8 fresh McIntosh apples (from winter to late summer, use Granny Smith apples as they stay fresh longer)
½ cup sugar
⅛ teaspoon salt
⅛ teaspoon ground nutmeg
1 teaspoon ground cinnamon
Pinch of ground allspice
1 tablespoon freshly squeezed lemon juice
Piecrusts for one 9-inch pie
   (Barry uses Pillsbury Pie Crusts)
4 tablespoons (½ stick) unsalted butter,
   cut into ½-inch pieces

1. Preheat the oven to 400°F.

2. Peel and core the apples and slice into ¾-inch wedges. (If using Granny Smith apples, slice into ½-inch wedges.)

3. In a large bowl, toss the apple pieces with the sugar, salt, nutmeg, cinnamon, allspice, and lemon juice.

4. Roll out the bottom piecrust thinly and place in the bottom of a 9-inch ovenproof pie dish.

5. Place the seasoned apples on the crust, mounding them up in the center. Dot the top of the apple filling with the butter pieces.

6. Roll out the top piecrust thinly and place over the apple filling. Pinch the edges of the crusts together. With a sharp knife, pierce the top crust in a few places so that air can escape.

7. Bake for 15 minutes, then lower the oven temperature to 350°F and continue baking for another 35 minutes, until the apples are cooked through. Serve at room temperature.

Terry's Chocolate Hazelnut Mousse Cake

Terry Moore, the owner-chef of The Old Mill restaurant in South Egremont, Massachusetts, has served this sumptuous cake for many years.

Time: 6 hours, including resting time
Serves 10 to 12

Butter for parchment paper
4 large eggs, at room temperature
½ cup granulated sugar
¼ cup unbleached all-purpose flour
⅔ cup good-quality baking (unsweetened) cocoa
Pinch of salt
1 tablespoon pure vanilla extract
One 13-ounce jar Nutella
One 8-ounce container chocolate hazelnut butter
    (preferably Tierra Farm)
One 8-ounce container mascarpone cheese
1 envelope unflavored gelatin
½ cup superfine sugar
3¾ cups heavy cream, chilled, plus extra whipped cream
    for serving
6 ounces bittersweet chocolate chips

Note: Tierra Farm products are available at Guido's Fresh Marketplace in Great Barrington, Massachusetts, and online at tierrafarm.com.

OPPOSITE: The dessert table, in a corner of the kitchen. We kept the desserts in a cooler room until the guests were finished eating the main course. When we wheeled the table out, there was a chorus of "ahhhhs."

1. Preheat the oven to 350°F.

2. To make the chocolate sponge cake: Place a buttered parchment paper circle inside a 9-inch springform cake pan. In the bowl of a stand mixer with whisk attachment, whisk the eggs at high speed for 8 minutes. Sift together the granulated sugar, flour, ⅓ cup of the cocoa, and the salt. Gradually add the dry ingredients to the beaten eggs and mix. Add the vanilla and mix again. Pour the mixture into the cake pan and bake for about 25 minutes, until the center is firm to the touch. Place the pan on a wire rack to cool.

3. To make the chocolate hazelnut mousse: Individually warm the Nutella, hazelnut butter, and mascarpone in a microwave, then combine all three ingredients in a mixing bowl. Dissolve the gelatin in ¼ cup cold water by warming the mixture in the microwave or on the stovetop until absorbed. Fold the gelatin into the Nutella mixture. Combine the superfine sugar, the remaining ⅓ cup cocoa, and 3 cups of the cream in the bowl of an electric mixer, whisking until firm. Fold into the Nutella mixture, then pour the mixture over the cooled sponge cake in the springform pan. With a long spatula, dome the top of the mousse. Place the pan, covered with plastic wrap, in the refrigerator for 4 hours.

4. To make the chocolate ganache: Heat the remaining ¾ cup cream in a small saucepan just until it begins to simmer, then pour it over the chocolate chips in a bowl and let stand for 5 minutes. With a wooden spoon, stir the mixture for a few minutes until it is smooth and glossy.

5. To assemble the dessert: Unmold the mousse cake, remove it from the base, discard the parchment paper, and place the cake on a wire rack over a large tray to collect the extra ganache. In a steady stream, pour the ganache over the cake, starting from the center and working out to the edges. Let the ganache flow down to coat the sides of the cake. Let cool in the refrigerator for 30 minutes or longer. Serve with plenty of whipped cream.

BREAKFAST SCHOOL

MENU

*Egg in a Hole

*Grilled Sausages and
Tomatoes

Sautéed Mushrooms

Drew Evans is a recent convert to country life. After sixteen years living in Manhattan, working as a professional fund-raiser, he gave it all up and relocated to a former schoolhouse in a small village in Columbia County. And then, looking for part-time work, he wandered into one of the Hammertown stores and began a new career selling home furnishings. It wasn't as radical a change as it might seem: Drew grew up in rural England in a farming village, in a landscape similar to his present one.

The old schoolhouse is now a cozy, stylish refuge for Drew and his two friendly Boston terriers, Iris and Junior. Built in 1840, the house still has the original door and the bell tower. It functioned as a schoolhouse for more than one hundred years; then it was used as a town hall. Drew is the first person in all those years to use the building as a residence, and it suits him perfectly. He added needed space upstairs, raising the ceilings in the bedrooms and opening up a view to the woods in back. Drew's many collections—photographs, mounted taxidermy, books—are displayed on the walls. He had long collected old educational charts, including maps and botanicals: They are perfectly at home in this former school building.

When friends come up for the weekend, Drew treats them to a proper English breakfast, featuring sausages, tomatoes, mushrooms, and Drew's version of toad-in-the-hole. Liberal pourings of champagne and fresh orange juice start the feast, with plenty of strong coffee to follow.

Tomatoes and bread, ready to go. Every kitchen should have a large serrated knife for slicing bread and tomatoes. Cutting boards come in many materials; this slate one is from Hammertown.

The original front door of this former schoolhouse, with morning light streaming through the transom and a row of wooden pegs at the ready for coats and mufflers. OPPOSITE: Drew has long collected old schoolroom maps and charts, which are happily at home in their new setting. OVERLEAF, LEFT: The vintage dining table has a zinc top and came from Hammertown Barn; RIGHT: Sturdy white plates from Fishs Eddy, with vintage wood-handled table knives.

TIPS

Sunday breakfast in the country is a special occasion. It's more relaxed than the weekday meal, and while it doesn't last all day—that meal is called brunch—it's a leisurely occasion. The fare is hearty enough to fuel a full country day of nature walks and exploring antiques shops.

Being served local farm produce is a special treat for urban visitors.

Egg in a Hole

This Americanized twist on the traditional British toad-in-the-hole—which involves sausage and Yorkshire pudding batter—is simpler and lighter.

Time: 20 minutes
Serves 6

1 round loaf peasant bread, thickly sliced
1 tablespoon olive oil
1 tablespoon unsalted butter
6 large eggs
Sea salt and freshly ground black pepper

1. Cut a round hole using a shot glass or small glass jar, about 1½ inches in diameter, in each slice of bread.

2. Heat 1 teaspoon of the olive oil and 1 teaspoon of the butter in a nonstick saucepan over medium heat. When the butter has melted, place a slice of bread on the surface.

3. When the bread begins to brown, break an egg into the hole, keeping the yoke from breaking. (This is easier to do if you break the egg into a little bowl first.) Season with salt and pepper. When the egg has cooked enough that the underside is firm, about 2 minutes, turn it over to briefly cook on the other side. When the egg white is set but the yolk is still runny, remove the toast to a warmed plate.

4. Repeat for the remaining 5 eggs, adding oil and butter to the pan by the teaspoon as needed. It's possible to cook 2 or 3 toasts at the same time.

5. Arrange on warmed plates and serve with the grilled sausages and tomatoes, and sautéed mushrooms.

Grilled Sausages and Tomatoes

The sausages were made from pasture-raised pork from Pigasso Farms, in nearby Copake, New York.

Time: 45 to 60 minutes
Serves 6

2 pounds fresh breakfast sausage links
3 whole ripe tomatoes
½ cup extra virgin olive oil
¼ cup balsamic vinegar
1 teaspoon dried herbes de Provence
¼ teaspoon sea salt
Freshly ground black pepper

1. Preheat the oven to 350°F.

2. Arrange the sausage links on a rack over a baking sheet. Prick them on all sides with a fork and place them in the oven.

3. Cut the tomatoes in half and arrange them, cut side up, on a parchment-lined baking sheet. In a small bowl, combine the olive oil, balsamic vinegar, herbs, and salt. Drizzle the mixture over the tomatoes, adding pepper to taste. Place the tomatoes in the oven.

4. Check the oven after 45 minutes. When the sausages are cooked through and the tomatoes are brown and bubbling on top, remove them from the oven and arrange them on warmed plates.

OPPOSITE, TOP LEFT: Colorful eggs from free-range chickens.

A WARM DINNER FOR A COLD NIGHT

MENU

STARTER
*Pizza with Artichoke Hearts
and Agrodolce

FIRST COURSE
*Butternut Squash Soup

MAIN
*Osso Buco

SIDES
*Celery Root and Potato Mash
Broccoli Rabe Sauté

DESSERT
*Cream Cheese and
Blueberry Pound Cake

"Life curated" is the motto for Finch, Andrew Arrick and Michael Hofemann's stylish shop on antiques row in Hudson, New York. (*The New York Times* called it "an artfully conceived and expansive home store.") The phrase could also apply to their country home, a rambling 1700s house that was once an inn. Andrew and Michael are both longtime veterans of the design and fashion worlds. When they bought the house in 2013, it needed some repairs, but other than paint they respected its original features, like the intricately joined beadboard work on the ceiling of the dining room. "Nothing in this house is perfect; everything's a bit wonky," Andrew says. Antiques, vintage pieces, original art, and midcentury Scandinavian design are all at home here. On winter nights the house comes to life with candlelight, laughter, and delicious cooking smells.

We caught up with Andrew and Michael on one such occasion, and watched as Andrew prepared dinner for six friends, from scratch. The kitchen is a mix of old and new, with original cabinetry, repurposed marble slabs as countertops, and a workhorse six-burner restaurant stove. A big blackboard on one wall still displayed a garden plan and lists of the vegetables that Michael grows on sixteen raised beds—now resting under a thick blanket of snow—outside. From last summer's harvest, Andrew cut up butternut squash for soup. While the soup was cooking, he started the main course, osso buco, on top of the stove. On another burner, big chunks of celery root and potato boiled away. Half an hour before the guests were due to arrive, he assembled the pizza hors d'oeuvre. Then, while the guests were finishing the soup, he quickly sautéed the broccoli rabe in olive oil. The osso buco came out to well-earned fanfare. One of the guests provided the dessert. It was a simple but soul-satisfying meal for a cold winter's night.

Andrew and Michael set their table with lovingly collected dishes and flatware. The antique silver is from a set that was a wedding gift to Andrew's parents from his grandparents.

LEFT: Matilda, the dog, snoozes beneath a Swedish floor clock that was a gift from Andrew's father, who was an antiques dealer in Newport, Rhode Island. BELOW: The entry hall, with a nineteenth-century bench from India. OPPOSITE: The living room contains an eclectic mix of antiques and midcentury modern. The portrait is by Russian-American artist Isaac Soyer (1902–1981). The faux bois wall sconces are French, from the 1920s.

TIPS

Having a well-stocked pantry takes a lot of the stress out of entertaining.

Always taste food just before serving, no matter how rushed you are. Does it need more salt? A quick squeeze of lemon juice?

A dollop of butter works wonders in a too-thin sauce, while a pinch of sugar can tame an overly bitter dish.

What makes an appetizer appetizing? It should entice, waken the taste buds, and create expectation. It's a chance to be adventurous, to try out bolder flavors.

The dining room, aglow with candlelight and party spirit. The farm table originally belonged to a woodworker and bears the scars and burns of hard use. The wallpaper is from Farrow & Ball; the intricate metal wall sconces were another gift from Andrew's dad. The ceramic urn behind the table comes from the renowned French pottery brand Astier de Valette.

1. Peppers,
2. Beat, Carr...
3. Tomato
4. Peppers (hot), Onion
5. Arugula, Spinach
6. Rutabega, Fennel, Broccoli, Eggplant
7. Parsnip, Turnip, Swiss Chard
8. Tomato
9. Tomato, Collard Greens
10. Lettuce
11. Cabbage, Brussels Sprouts
12. Summer Squash
13. Hot Peppers, Celery, Celeriac
14. Zucchini
15. Kale
16. Potato...

Sides
S: Winter Squash, Beens, Cucumber
W: Herbs, Cucumber
W.D. Melon Patch

The kitchen is both a delight to the eye and an efficient working space.
ABOVE LEFT: Remembrance of summer past—on the chalkboard, lists of the
vegetables Michael grows in sixteen large raised beds. ABOVE RIGHT: The
antique sink came from a shop in Hudson, New York. The countertop is
made of reclaimed marble slabs. OPPOSITE: The floor cloth and the
wonderful old pot rack came from estate sales in Newport, Rhode Island.

Pizza with Artichoke Hearts and Agrodolce

This tasty hors d'oeuvre, using ingredients from the pantry, came together quickly. Andrew buys the fig agrodolce, a tangy-sweet conserve, and the pizza dough at Adams Fairacre Farms in Lake Katrine, near Kingston, New York; these items can also be found at specialty food shops.

Time: ¹⁄₂ hour
Serves 10

Spray oil
2 tablespoons olive oil
1 large onion, very thinly sliced (1 cup)
1 pound prepared pizza dough, at room temperature
¹⁄₂ cup fig agrodolce
¹⁄₂ cup canned artichoke hearts,
   drained and roughly chopped
1 cup coarsely grated Gruyère cheese
Freshly ground black pepper

1. Preheat the oven to 450° F.

2. Heat the olive oil in a medium saucepan and cook the onions slowly over low heat until they are well caramelized. Set them aside.

3. Coat a 10 by 14-inch baking sheet with cooking oil spray.

4. Stretch the pizza dough and spread it evenly on the baking sheet. Using a fork, prick the dough all over to prevent air bubbles.

5. Spread the agrodolce on the dough. Top with the caramelized onions, then the artichoke hearts, and the Gruyère. Sprinkle with pepper. Place the pizza in the hot oven and cook until nicely browned, about 15 minutes.

6. Cut the pizza into small rectangles and serve at once.

Andrew collects candlesticks; mixing the different shapes and styles makes for a lively display.

Butternut Squash Soup

The squash for this gorgeous golden soup came from last summer's garden.

Time: 1 hour
Serves 6

1 tablespoon unsalted butter
2 tablespoons good olive oil, plus more
    for drizzling
2 small onions, thinly sliced
1 medium tomato, diced
1 garlic clove, diced
½ teaspoon crushed red pepper flakes
3 cups low-sodium beef stock
2 pounds butternut squash, peeled and
    cut into 2-inch chunks
1 tablespoon kosher salt, plus more to taste
Freshly ground black pepper
Flat-leaf parsley for garnish

1. Heat the butter and olive oil in a small saucepan over low heat. Add the onions and tomato and cook slowly until the onions are soft and translucent, about 5 minutes. Add the garlic and red pepper flakes and cook briefly.

2. Deglaze the saucepan with ½ cup of the beef stock.

3. Transfer the contents of the saucepan to a large pot. Add the squash and cover with 2 cups water and the remaining 2½ cups stock. Add the salt. Bring the pot to a boil over a high heat.

4. Turn the heat down and let simmer, uncovered, until the squash is very soft, about 20 minutes.

5. Turn off the heat and, using an immersion blender, puree the squash until it has an even, creamy consistency. (This step may also be done in a blender or food processor.) Season with salt and pepper, and reheat if necessary. Serve in warmed soup bowls, topped with a drizzle of olive oil and parsley sprigs.

Osso buco is perfect winter's night fare. LEFT: A bottle of red wine added to the simmering vegetables. ABOVE: The finished dish.

Osso Buco

In Andrew's version of this classic Italian recipe, he uses red wine instead of the usual white.

Time: 3 hours
Serves 6

Six 2-inch pieces bone-in veal shanks
½ cup unbleached all-purpose flour
2 tablespoons good olive oil
2 tablespoons unsalted butter
1 cup onions, diced
½ cup carrots, thinly sliced
1 large celery stalk, thinly sliced (½ cup)
3 large garlic cloves, halved
½ cup fresh flat-leaf parsley, roughly chopped,
    plus some sprigs for garnish
Zest of 1 lemon peeled in 1-inch strips (be sure
    to avoid the pith, which is bitter tasting)
One 750-milliliter bottle good red wine
2 cups low-sodium beef stock
One 28-ounce can or container imported Italian
    whole peeled tomatoes, peeled and chopped,
    with juice reserved
2 bay leaves
Kosher salt and freshly ground black pepper

1. Preheat the oven to 375°F.

2. Dry the veal shanks with paper towels, then dredge them lightly in the flour.

3. Warm the olive oil and butter in a large Dutch oven or heavy-bottomed ovenproof casserole over medium heat. Add the veal shanks, turning them so they brown well on all sides, about 10 minutes. Remove the meat and set aside.

4. Add the onions, carrots, celery, garlic, parsley, and lemon zest to the pan. Over low heat, sweat the vegetables until they are soft and translucent. Add the wine and bring to a boil over high heat. When the wine is reduced by half, return the veal pieces to the pot and add the beef stock, tomatoes, and bay leaves. Transfer the pot to the oven and cook, covered, for about 2 hours, until the meat is very tender. Remove the bay leaves. Season with salt and pepper and serve with generous spoonings of sauce.

Celery Root and Potato Mash

Adding celery root to the potatoes takes this dish to another level.

Time: 1 hour
Serves 6 to 8

3 whole celery roots, peeled and cut up
    into 1-inch cubes (about 3 cups)
3 large potatoes (Yukon gold or russets), peeled and
    cut up into 1-inch cubes (about 3 cups)
8 tablespoons (1 stick) unsalted butter,
    plus extra as needed
Kosher salt and freshly ground black pepper
1 cup whole milk Greek yogurt

1. Put the celery root and potato pieces in a large pot, cover with plenty of water, and bring to a boil. Reduce the heat and simmer, uncovered, for about 20 minutes.

2. When the vegetables are cooked through, drain off most of the water. Add the butter, and salt and pepper to taste. Using a potato masher, mash until the consistency is smooth. Add more butter as needed.

3. At serving time, reheat. Whisk together with the yogurt.

Cream Cheese and Blueberry Pound Cake

Guest Ted Saad brought this luscious cake to the dinner party: The recipe came from his friend Melissa Macaluso.

Time: 2 hours
Serves 6 to 8

1½ cups unbleached all-purpose flour
½ teaspoon baking powder
½ teaspoon salt
3½ ounces cream cheese, at room temperature
8 tablespoons (1 stick) unsalted butter, at room
    temperature, plus extra for greasing the pan
1½ cups sugar

4 large eggs, at room temperature
1 teaspoon pure vanilla extract
1 teaspoon freshly grated lemon zest
1 teaspoon freshly grated orange zest
1 cup blueberries, fresh or frozen
1 cup whipped cream
1 cup fresh strawberries, cut in half

1. Preheat the oven to 325° F.

2. Combine the flour, baking powder, and salt in a large bowl. Stir to blend.

3. In the bowl of a stand mixer with a paddle attachment, beat the cream cheese and butter until very pale and little tails form. Add the sugar and beat until fluffy. Scrape the sides of the bowl and add the eggs, one at a time, beating well after each addition.

4. Add the vanilla, lemon zest, and orange zest to the flour mixture and transfer the contents of the bowl to the mixer. With the mixer on low speed, briefly combine all the ingredients. Finish with a stiff rubber spatula and mix until smooth. Gently fold in the blueberries.

5. Grease an 8 by 5-inch loaf pan with plenty of butter. Scrape the batter into the pan and bake in the middle of the oven for 60 to 65 minutes (or 75 to 90 minutes if using frozen berries), until the cake is golden brown and a toothpick inserted into the center comes out clean. Cool the pan on a rack for 15 minutes, then invert the pan and lightly tap to release the cake.

6. Cool the cake completely on the rack before serving. Serve with the whipped cream and strawberries.

Wide drawers in the dining table provide storage for a collection of old napkins. Andrew is partial to those monogrammed with the initial A. The chair seats are made from vintage German grain sacks.

A TOAST TO SPRING

MENU

Red and White Wine,
Sparkling Water

Assorted Cheeses with
Breads and Crackers

Dried Fruits and Nuts

*Prosciutto-Wrapped
Asparagus Spears

Designers, landscapers, and antiques collectors have been beating a path to Michael Trapp's eponymous store in West Cornwall, Connecticut, for more than twenty-five years. Just over the covered bridge in this picture-perfect New England village, the shop, in a building that dates to the 1820s and had been used as a garage before Michael took it on, is surrounded by a rigorously pruned and terraced three-quarter-acre garden. If not for the snow, it would feel like Tuscany. Michael's taste is both impeccable and wonderfully quirky. Fragments of classical statuary share shelf space with flowering orchids, bones and shells, exotic textiles, jewelry, vintage tableware, and precious furnishings. The mix changes constantly. Michael closes the shop at the end of the summer season and spends the winter months traveling the world buying wonderful things. On the first day of spring he celebrates the reopening of the store with a big party.

We came early to watch the preparations. Snow still lay thickly on the ground outdoors, but inside the atmosphere was warm and festive. The shop's rooms were full of new finds, gleaned from Michael's winter travels to Peru, Indonesia, Cambodia, and Paris. One to two hundred guests were expected. An artist friend, Rachel Schwarz, artfully arranged dried fruits and nuts (ordered online from nuts.com) on platters, while another friend put together an asparagus hors d'oeuvre. As the guests arrived, they wandered through the rooms, admiring this year's harvest of treasures. The main bar was set up at one end of the house, in the garden room, with a second bar in the kitchen, and hors d'oeuvres shared table space with the antiques and objets. There was a happy buzz as friends greeted one another. Wine flowed; the season had begun.

Getting ready for the party: On the massive kitchen table, cheeses and bags of nuts and dried fruits will be turned into elegant hors d'ouevres. OVERLEAF: There are two bar setups, at the opposite ends of the house, in the kitchen (top left) and the main bar (opposite), in the garden room; (BOTTOM LEFT) wine chilling outside in fresh snow.

TIPS

How much wine to buy for a party? A good general rule is to have one-half bottle of wine for each guest—a case of wine will serve twenty-four guests—and then add another 20 percent.

People drink more white wine in the summer, more red in the winter; it's good to have lots of both. Leftover unopened bottles can be put aside for the next occasion or, possibly, returned to the liquor store. (Ask ahead of time.) Don't stint.

Many fine wines are now bottled in twist-off caps, which is a great convenience for a self-service bar.

Have plenty of ice on hand, as well as still and sparkling water.

TOP LEFT: A cabinet holds and displays table linens. LEFT: This little dish, one of Michael's recent finds, comes from an ancient shipwreck. ABOVE: A simple, quickly assembled hors d'ouevre: slices of cured ham with Gruyère cheese on whole wheat crackers. OPPOSITE: A beautiful glass urn chock-full of dried and fresh fruits.

Michael's friend, Rachel Schwarz, arranged Jarlsberg, Gouda, and Gruyère cheeses and other treats in colorful patterns on serving platters. They were displayed along with the artifacts and antiques that Michael brought back to Connecticut from distant shores. OVERLEAF, LEFT: There are potted plants and flowers everywhere in this house, all a part of the Michael Trapp world.

Prosciutto-Wrapped Asparagus Spears

Michael's friend Mary Dzenutis has perfected this elegant hors d'oeuvre, which she generously contributed to the party. For best results, use nice thick asparagus spears.

Time: 1 hour
Serves 10 to 20 as an hors d'oeuvre or 6 as a first course

2 pounds thick asparagus spears
1 pound good-quality prosciutto

1. Trim the asparagus: Discard the thick ends of the stems and, using a vegetable peeler, scrape away the tough skins. The asparagus spears should all be approximately the same length.

2. Place the asparagus in one layer in a large pan of warm water. Cover the pan with a lid or aluminum foil and bring to a boil. Turn off the heat and leave the asparagus in the hot water for 2 minutes, until they are tender but still firm. Then drain them and quickly rinse with cold water.

3. Unwrap the prosciutto and place it flat on a baking sheet in the freezer for 5 minutes, to make for easier handling.

4. Roll each asparagus spear in a slice of prosciutto. Arrange the slices on a round platter in a wheel, with the green tips pointing out. Use a few smaller spears to garnish the center. Refrigerate until ready to serve.

A NEIGHBORLY GET-TOGETHER

MENU

BEVERAGE
*Rhubarb Spritzer

MAIN
*Chicken Potpie

SIDES
*Roasted Asparagus
*Green Salad with
Julia's Vinaigrette

DESSERT
*Semifreddo with Strawberries

On an unexpectedly warm spring evening, Julia Turshen and Grace Bonney invited some of their neighbors to join them for dinner in their new/old Hudson Valley home. Julia is a rising star in the professional food world: She has coauthored eight cookbooks with such luminaries as Gwyneth Paltrow and Mario Batali, and now has published a book of her own, *Small Victories*. Her wife, Grace, is the founder of the influential blog Design*Sponge and the author of *Design*Sponge at Home* and *In the Company of Women*. Former died-in-the-wool urbanites, they were as surprised as everyone else when they became full-time country dwellers not long after their November 2013 wedding. Looking for a weekend getaway, they found a rambling, circa 1830s, former boardinghouse in New York's Ulster County. The relaxing rural quiet and lack of big city distractions made for an inspiring work environment, and they soon decided to make the country their year-round residence. Getting through their first harsh winter only confirmed their commitment to the rustic life. They decorated the house, incorporating heirlooms from both their families: Grace threw herself into gardening, Julia discovered local sources for meat and produce, and they began entertaining.

Dinner at the Bonney-Turshen home is a treat for all the senses. The large country kitchen includes a windowed dining alcove with a custom-built banquette. After guests arrive, they sip Julia's original aperitifs and watch—and sometimes help—as she prepares the meal, while Grace arranges flowers and treasured linens on the long table.

Julia grew up in a style-conscious home. Both parents were book designers and worked with the late Lee Bailey: The iconic cookbook author, designer, and tastemaker was—and is still—an important influence. His simple but elegant recipes, attention to detail, and love of entertaining have inspired Julia's career. In an article in *Saveur* magazine (March 2016), Julia wrote that Bailey "was a pioneer in suggesting that a meal's setting was as important as the food." Julia and Grace honor this philosophy every day.

The table is set with pretty china plates, vintage linens, and lilacs from the garden.
The food will be passed around and the guests will serve themselves.

LUNCH
Now BEING
SERVED

OPPOSITE: In a cozy sitting room close to the kitchen, a vintage sign is a playful reminder of the importance of food and hospitality to Julia and Grace. CLOCKWISE, FROM TOP LEFT: This built-in cupboard with wainscoting, a copper countertop, and vintage hardware holds frequently used dishware and supplies. The giant whisk was a gift from Julia's father, Doug Turshen. In the garden, an oversize hammock and a couple of low wooden chairs encourage outdoor living. Winky, the dog, stands inside the screen door, ready to welcome dinner guests.

Rhubarb Spritzer

This is an unusual and very refreshing seasonal aperitif. Rhubarb is at its best between April and June.

Time: 1 hour
Makes 4 cocktails

3 rhubarb stalks
$\frac{1}{2}$ cup sugar
1 cup good-quality gin
1 cup Campari
2 cups sparkling water
1 lemon, cut in half

1. Cut the rhubarb stalks into $\frac{1}{2}$-inch slices, put them in a medium saucepan with 1 cup water and the sugar, and cook over medium heat until they are very soft. Strain the mixture into a bowl, discarding the rhubarb pulp. Set aside to cool.

2. Combine the rhubarb juice with the gin, Campari, sparkling water, and the juice of half a lemon. Pour into a pitcher with ice in it.

3. Serve the cocktail in chilled glasses with ice, garnished with lemon slices from the other half of the lemon.

The bar, with vintage glasses and an assortment of beverages, is assembled on a high counter that divides the kitchen from the dining area. Julia's Rhubarb Spritzer is served in a pitcher. Sliced lemons and limes are at the ready, and there are nuts and olives for nibbling while enjoying a drink.

Chicken Potpie

Julia's recipe yields a savory one-dish meal that is comfort food elevated to new heights of flavor. Using crème fraîche instead of béchamel is an ingenious shortcut. She buys organically raised, free-run chickens from local farmers; the taste is incomparable.

Time: 2 hours
Serves 6 to 8

For the crust
8 tablespoons (1 stick) cold unsalted butter, cut into small pieces
Pinch of salt
1¼ cups unbleached all-purpose flour

1. By hand or using a food processor, quickly combine the butter, salt, and flour until the mixture forms pea-size pieces.

2. Add ½ cup ice water, by teaspoonfuls, until the mixture just sticks together. Shape the dough into a ball, then flatten it into a disk. Wrap in plastic wrap and refrigerate for at least 30 minutes. (This can be done ahead of time.)

For the completed pie
6 bone-in, skin-on chicken breasts, cooked (Julia roasts them the night before)
One 10-ounce package small frozen peas, defrosted at room temperature
1 cup finely diced shallots
2 tablespoons Dijon mustard
8 ounces crème fraîche
½ teaspoon freshly ground black pepper
1 teaspoon Maldon sea salt flakes
Extra virgin olive oil for greasing the pan
1 tablespoon unbleached all-purpose flour for flouring the parchment paper
1 large egg, beaten

1. Preheat the oven to 375°F.

2. Shred the chicken, removing and discarding the skin and bones. The meat should be in bite-size pieces.

3. Combine the shredded chicken with the peas and shallots in a large bowl. Add the mustard, crème fraîche, pepper, and ½ teaspoon of the salt. Mix well.

4. Transfer the chicken mixture to an olive oil–greased 12-inch ovenproof pan.

5. On a floured sheet of parchment paper, roll out the refrigerated dough, turning it several times, until it is ¼ inch thick and slightly larger than the pan. Use the parchment paper to lift the dough and unroll it on top of the chicken filling; discard the paper. Pinch the edges.

6. Brush the surface of the dough with the beaten egg, then sprinkle with the remaining ½ teaspoon salt. Make slits in the dough so that steam can escape.

7. Cook the pie on a baking sheet for 45 minutes, or until the crust is nicely browned and the filling is bubbling. Serve hot.

TIPS

Julia finds many uses for parchment paper: She uses it to roll out pie dough and to line baking pans. Parchment paper is nontoxic, nonconductive, and makes for very easy cleanup.

Julia buys parchment paper precut into squares online from King Arthur Flour (kingarthurflour.com). Online shopping is a great convenience when you live in a rural area.

Julia assembles her Chicken Potpie; it's fascinating to watch an accomplished cook at work. TOP, LEFT AND RIGHT: The shredded chicken, in a bowl with crème fraîche and mustard; a shower of chopped shallots. MIDDLE ROW AND BOTTOM: Assembling the piecrust. OPPOSITE: The final touch: cutting slits in the crust so steam can escape.

Roasted Asparagus

Spring is asparagus time in the Northeast. Early in April asparagus spears begin pushing their way up through the ground. For a few precious weeks they are abundantly available locally in farmers' markets and on dinner tables. This easy recipe celebrates that moment.

Time: 30 minutes
Serves 6 to 8

2 pounds fresh asparagus
3 to 4 tablespoons extra virgin olive oil
1 teaspoon kosher salt
1 lemon, cut up in wedges for garnish

1. Preheat the oven to 400°F.

2. Cut off the tough ends of the asparagus spears. Spread them in one layer on two baking sheets lined with parchment paper. Sprinkle with the olive oil and salt.

3. Roast for 15 minutes. Serve at room temperature, with lemon wedges.

Time: 5 minutes
Makes 1 cup

1 tablespoon Dijon mustard
⅓ cup sherry vinegar
2 tablespoons finely diced shallots
½ teaspoon kosher salt
⅔ cup extra virgin olive oil
2 teaspoons honey
Freshly ground black pepper, to taste

Combine the mustard, vinegar, shallots, salt, olive oil, honey, and pepper in a 10-ounce jar with a lid and shake well until emulsified.

Note: This dressing can be made ahead of time and will keep for at least a week, refrigerated. Shake well before using.

Green Salad with Julia's Vinaigrette

This refreshing salad is the perfect counterpoint to Julia's hearty chicken potpie.

Time: 15 minutes
Serves 6

2 bunches fresh young salad greens, washed and dried
1 cup fresh tomatoes, quartered
1 cup Julia's Vinaigrette (recipe follows)
5 scallions, trimmed and cut into ⅛-inch slices

1. Tear the greens into bite-size pieces and place in a serving bowl. Add the tomatoes.

2. Pour the vinaigrette over the greens and gently toss. Garnish the salad with the scallion slices and serve at once.

To end the dinner, a luscious cold dessert, Semifreddo with Strawberries, is served on a color-coordinated red-rimmed plate.

Semifreddo with Strawberries

Semifreddo is Italian for "half-cold." This delectable dessert is surprisingly easy to prepare, and makes for a sensational presentation.

Time: 15 minutes, plus at least 6 hours
(up to 24 hours) in the freezer
Serves 6 to 8

1 pint good-quality vanilla ice cream
½ cup heavy cream, stiffly whipped
1 pound fresh strawberries, hulled and
    cut into ¼-inch slices
1 tablespoon sugar
Juice of ½ lemon

1. Let the ice cream soften slightly at room temperature so that it can be spooned.

2. Fold the softened ice cream together with the whipped cream. Pack the ice cream mixture into a small loaf pan lined with plastic wrap. Cover in plastic wrap, and freeze for at least 6 hours.

3. Stir the strawberries together with the sugar and lemon juice.

4. Remove the ice cream loaf from the freezer. Slip a table knife under the plastic wrap to loosen the ice cream loaf. Discard the plastic wrap. Using a heated knife, slice the loaf into 1-inch servings. Top with the strawberries and serve.

A PERFECT DAY FOR A PICNIC

"You have to be a little imperfect to be perfect." This is Patrick Robinson's philosophy, which he applies to his work as a fashion designer, and to the simple, imaginative meals he cooks for his family. His wife, Virginia Smith, is the fashion market/accessories director at *Vogue*, and they have a young son, Wyeth. During the week (when Virginia isn't in Milan, Paris, or London) they race about New York City, going to meetings and fashion shows, accompanying Wyeth to and from school and to his after-school activities. But on weekends they put it all behind them and relax at their Hudson Valley home. This corner of New York's Columbia County is pastoral, with rolling hills, farmland, and lots of open sky. The house, which was originally a barn, had already been converted when Virginia and Patrick found it. They've done some remodeling, opening up windows and building decks. The interior is casual but refined; Virginia cites Belgian designer Axel Vervoordt as an inspiration. There are rough beams, clean-lined modern furniture, and piles of books. Outside, there's a big vegetable garden, a family of chickens, a pond with a weeping willow, and a great old oak tree, the setting for many summer picnics.

Patrick is the family cook. He moves easily and confidently around the big open kitchen, cleaning up as he works. Today's meal is mostly sourced locally, and it celebrates the season. The herbs, salad greens, and flowers for the table all come from their backyard. As Patrick cooks, the guests sip rosé and chat with Wyeth. Virginia loads the food and wine and the table settings onto a wagon and pulls it down to the picnic table, under the oak tree. As the sun moves overhead, family and friends linger over lunch, chickens clucking in the background, punctuated by an occasional raucous cock-a-doodle-doo. The meal concludes with bite-size strawberry tarts, from Taart Work Pies in Brooklyn. They are garnished with organic strawberries picked earlier in the day at nearby Thompson-Finch Farm.

This magnificent old oak tree provides shade and shelter for a summer afternoon in the country. The peonies were picked earlier in the day.

CLOCKWISE FROM TOP RIGHT: Virginia uses an all-purpose garden wagon to haul the table settings from the house to the picnic site. The rooster protects a family of chickens that provide eggs for the kitchen. The vegetable garden is well fenced to keep out deer and other marauders. Windows flanking the front door bring light through the house. OPPOSITE: Patrick built the decks that surround two sides of this former barn. In the foreground, grapevines climb a trellis outside the garden.

TIP

It takes some planning to maintain a kitchen in a weekend house. Patrick and Virginia keep their pantry stocked with the usual basics: flour, sugar, salt, coffee, tea, spices, dried herbs, oil, vinegar, dried beans, pasta, canned goods, and much more. Patrick stores leftover chicken bones in Ziploc bags in the freezer. The bottom line is that if all else fails, they can put together a meal from the larder.

Patrick mans the stove. This kitchen, with its rough beams, restaurant range, and ample workspace, was one of the selling points of the house. Patrick and Virginia added the stylish light fixture above the table.

LEFT: The guests enjoy a pre lunch sip of rosé, while catching up with Wyeth, Patrick and Virginia's eleven-year-old son. BELOW AND OPPOSITE: The two-story living room, with its comfortable seating and book-strewn coffee table, is at the center of the house.

Flatbread Pizza

Who doesn't love pizza? Patrick's recipe makes a hearty rustic pizza that is perfect picnic food.

Time: 1½ hours
Serves 8

1 pound fresh cherry tomatoes
4 garlic cloves, finely diced
4 shallots, finely diced
¼ cup extra virgin olive oil,
   plus extra for greasing the pan
1 teaspoon kosher salt
Freshly ground black pepper
2 flatbread crusts (Patrick uses Damascus
   Bakeries' Brooklyn Bred brand)
¼ cup shredded whole milk mozzarella cheese
½ cup ricotta cheese

1. Preheat the oven to 300°F.

2. Toss the tomatoes with the garlic, shallots, olive oil, salt, and pepper in a medium bowl.

3. Spread the seasoned tomatoes in a baking pan and roast them for 1 hour. Halfway through the cooking time, toss them again so they cook evenly. Remove the tomatoes from the oven and set aside.

4. Twenty minutes before serving time, turn the broiler on to high.

5. Place the flatbread crusts on a greased 10 by 18-inch baking sheet and spread the mozzarella and ricotta on top. Spoon the roasted tomatoes over the cheeses.

6. Place the pizzas under the broiler and cook for 10 to 12 minutes, until they are bubbling and the crusts are just beginning to brown. Cut into 2-inch slices and serve hot.

Baked Chicken with Olives

Like most of the ingredients at Patrick and Virginia's luncheon, the chickens used for this recipe are local, from the all-organic Herondale Farm just down the road from their house.

Time: 2 hours
Serves 8

Two 3-pound chickens, cut into 8 pieces
½ cup extra virgin olive oil (Patrick buys French
    olive oil at Bizalion's Fine Food in
    Great Barrington, Massachusetts)
1 medium onion, sliced
One 2-inch piece fresh ginger, finely minced
2 garlic cloves, finely minced
2 cinnamon sticks
1 tablespoon ground turmeric
2 cups good chicken stock
4 tablespoons green olives, pitted and roughly chopped
Kosher salt and freshly ground black pepper
1 cup fresh cilantro leaves and stems, coarsely chopped

1. Preheat the oven to 350°F.

2. Sauté the chicken pieces in ¼ cup of the olive oil in a large sauté pan over high heat until they are nicely browned on all sides. (You may have to do this in batches, or in more than one pan.) Transfer the chicken pieces to a large ovenproof pan.

3. Wipe the sauté pan with a paper towel to remove any burned bits. Add the remaining ¼ cup olive oil and cook the onion with the ginger and garlic over medium heat. When the onion begins to turn translucent, add the cinnamon sticks, turmeric, and chicken stock to the pan. Cook over high heat until the sauce is reduced by half.

4. Add the chopped olives to the sauce and pour the sauce over the chicken. Season with salt and pepper. Place the pan in the oven and cook until the chicken is thoroughly done (test with a fork to make sure the meat is no longer pink), about 15 minutes.

5. Garnish the finished dish with cilantro and serve.

Salad of Cauliflower, Broccoli, Asparagus, and Baby Greens

This satisfying salad combines hearty vegetables with fresh-from-the-garden greens and herbs.

Time: 1 hour
Serves 8

1 pound cauliflower, cut into florets
1 pound broccoli, cut into florets
1 pound asparagus, cut into 2-inch pieces
2 cups fresh young greens, such as arugula, spinach, or baby lettuce, washed and dried
$\frac{1}{4}$ cup fresh chives, chopped
$\frac{1}{4}$ cup chopped fresh herbs, such as flat-leaf parsley, tarragon, or chervil
Patrick Robinson's Salad Dressing (recipe follows)
$\frac{1}{4}$ cup chive flowers (if available) for garnish

1. Put a large pot of water over high heat and bring to a boil. When the water is fully boiling, drop the cauliflower and broccoli florets into the water and cover the pot briefly so that the water continues to boil.

2. After 2 minutes, use a slotted spoon to remove the vegetables to a colander in the sink, and run cold water over them for 2 minutes to chill.

3. Bring the water back to a boil and repeat the process with the asparagus pieces. When the asparagus is chilled, combine it with the cauliflower and broccoli florets in a large bowl.

4. Gently tear the greens into bite-size pieces. Add them to the chilled vegetables and sprinkle the chives and herbs over all.

5. Just before serving, add the salad dressing and lightly toss together. Garnish with chive flowers, if using.

OPPOSITE: The blanched vegetables will be dressed with Patrick's salad dressing and garnished with chive flowers just before serving. ABOVE RIGHT: Chives, tarragon, and basil from the garden. Chive flowers are both decorative and very tasty.

PATRICK'S SALAD DRESSING

Time: 5 minutes
Makes $\frac{3}{4}$ cup

Juice of 1 lemon
2 teaspoons apple cider vinegar
$\frac{1}{2}$ cup extra virgin olive oil
2 garlic cloves, minced
3 teaspoons sea salt
1 teaspoon freshly ground black pepper
1 teaspoon Dijon mustard

Combine the lemon juice, vinegar, olive oil, garlic, salt, pepper, and mustard in an 8-ounce glass jar with a lid. Shake vigorously to mix thoroughly.

Note: This dressing can be kept in the refrigerator for up to 2 weeks.

LEFT: The tarts are from Taartwork Pies in Brooklyn. Virginia says, "I love these cupcake-size strawberry pies—they're the perfect portion." OPPOSITE: Freshly picked organic strawberries from nearby Thompson-Finch Farm. They are grown without any chemicals and can be eaten right from the garden. Virginia drizzles balsamic vinegar on them: "It's an amazing combination."

SUNDAY AT HOME

MENU

BEVERAGES
Lemonade
Iced Tea

STARTER
*Cheese Plate

MAIN
*Grilled Steak
with Chimichurri Sauce

SIDES
*Salad of Snap Peas
and Ricotta Cheese

*Kale, Corn, and
Cherry Tomato Salad

DESSERT
Berry Pie

Dana and Jamey Simpson and their two preteen daughters, Lily and Olive, live in northwest Connecticut on a forty-acre wooded property just outside the picture-perfect village of Salisbury. Dana is an interior designer (who sometimes works with her mom, Joan Osofsky of Hammertown Barn), and Jamey manages real estate. As freelancers and parents, their lives are a busy whirl of errands and commitments, which are always centered on their home. The house has had several lives. Before the Simpsons bought it, it had been a weekend cottage and then an artist's studio. Remodeling—of the interior as well as the extensive grounds—is an ongoing project. The landscaping came first, and then the addition of porches and outside sitting areas; the interior, with a big, hardworking kitchen and lots of room for hobbies and collections, followed. The goal: an inside/outside home, child friendly and also grown-up friendly.

On a drizzly summer weekend afternoon, Dana and Jamey invited another couple, along with their two children, to share a midday feast. As the young ones wandered in and out, undaunted by the occasional showers, their elders chatted around a table at the end of the kitchen. Jamey and Dana are both accomplished cooks: Jamey's background includes culinary school and a stint owner-managing a restaurant. He and Dana share the chores, one doing prep work while the other stirs and cooks. Today the kids are ready to eat while the adults are still enjoying hors d'ouevres and conversation. Dana quickly puts together bowls of pasta for them, along with helpings of the two salads. In late afternoon the clouds clear in time for everyone to enjoy Jamey's chimichurri steak at the table outside, on the terrace. Berry pie—store-bought from nearby Sharon, Connecticut—caps the day.

The table is set for lunch on the terrace, close to the kitchen door.

The welcoming front porch: CLOCKWISE FROM RIGHT: The yellow door is adorned with a bunch of hydrangeas; a visiting dog makes himself at home; the wicker couch is piled with comfortable pillows.
OPPOSITE: This table, at one end of the kitchen, is a favorite family hangout. For the lunch it functions as a bar, where Dana will squeeze lemons for lemonade while chatting with the guests.

ABOVE: The cabinets and woodwork in the kitchen are painted Farrow & Ball's Green Blue. The kitchen was designed by architect Rafe Churchill. The round metal shape above the stove was originally a mold used in knife making.
OPPOSITE, LEFT AND RIGHT: Dana found this little demilune table at a local antiques shop. The custom-built cupboard holds dishes and glassware for everyday use.

Vintage wineglasses and sweet peas on an antique tole tray.

Cheese Plate

Dana assembles an eclectic assortment of cheeses and other treats, and arranges them on a platter with crisp crackers. The presentation is important, as is the balance of flavors.

Time: 15 minutes
Serves 6

½ cup pitted jarred picholine olives, with their juice
½ cup canned lupini beans, with their juice
    (Dana uses Victoria brand)
1 pound fine imported cheeses
1 pound crackers (Dana likes Jan's Farmhouse Crisps,
    a small artisanal brand from Vermont)
½ pound imported soppressata salami, thinly sliced
½ cup dried apricots
Jar of Dijon mustard

1. Combine the olives and beans, with their juices. Put them in a small bowl, with a fork for serving.

2. Unwrap the cheeses and arrange them on a board or platter, with the crackers, salami, apricots, the bowl of olives and beans, and the jar of mustard. Serve with cheese knives and cocktail napkins.

Note: Dana serves P'tit Basque cheese from Bizalion's Fine Food in Great Barrington, Massachusetts, and Italian Brunet cheese from LaBonne's Market, in Salisbury, Connecticut.

Grilled Steak with Chimichurri Sauce

Jamey marinates flank steak in a mixture of cilantro, parsley, and garlic; the result is intensely flavorful.

Time: 2½ hours
Serves 8

Special equipment: gas or charcoal grill

6 garlic cloves, crushed
¼ cup extra virgin olive oil
1 tablespoon kosher salt, plus more to taste
1 teaspoon freshly ground black pepper,
    plus more to taste
One 3-pound skirt steak, cut into 2 pieces
Chimichurri Sauce (recipe follows)

1. Put the garlic cloves, olive oil, salt, and pepper in a food processor or blender. Pulse the mixture a few times to combine all the ingredients. Pour the mixture into a 1-gallon resealable bag and add the steaks. Put the bag in the refrigerator and marinate for no longer than 2 hours.

2. Heat the grill: When the grill is very hot, remove the bag with the steaks from the refrigerator. Discard the marinade and cook the steaks on the grill for 2 minutes on each side. Remove them from the heat and allow them to rest for 5 minutes before serving.

3. Slice the steaks against the grain into 2-inch pieces and serve hot with the chimichurri sauce.

CHIMICHURRI SAUCE

Time: 5 minutes, plus 30 minutes resting time
Makes 2 cups

1 bunch fresh cilantro leaves and tender stems,
    washed, roughly chopped
1 cup fresh flat-leaf parsley leaves and tender stems,
    washed, roughly chopped
5 garlic cloves
Pinch of crushed red pepper flakes
½ teaspoon ground cumin
¼ cup red wine vinegar
½ teaspoon kosher salt
¼ teaspoon freshly ground black pepper
½ cup extra virgin olive oil

1. Put the cilantro, parsley, garlic, red pepper flakes, cumin, vinegar, salt, pepper, and olive oil in a food processor or blender and pulse, on and off, until the sauce thickens. Do not overprocess.

2. Transfer the sauce to a bowl and set aside for 30 minutes or more, so the flavors can blend. Stir before serving.

Vintage flatware, china, and striped cotton linens are stacked on the picnic table, in anticipation of the feast.

Salad of Snap Peas and Ricotta Cheese

This lovely salad is a Simpson-family favorite.

Time: 10 minutes
Serves 8

1 pound fresh sugar snap peas, trimmed
   (tails and strings removed)
¼ cup extra virgin olive oil
Grated zest of ½ lemon
¼ cup fresh mint leaves, cut into chiffonade
Sea salt and freshly ground black pepper
3 cups whole milk ricotta cheese

1. Bring a large pot of water to a boil and blanch the snap peas for 1 minute, then quickly transfer them to a bowl of cold water.

2. Whisk the olive oil with the lemon zest and mint in a small bowl. Drain the chilled snap peas and stir them together with the dressing. Season with salt and pepper.

3. Spread the ricotta on a serving dish. Pour the snap peas and dressing on top and serve at room temperature.

The gardens surrounding the house were designed by landscape designer Christine Krause; they combine strong geometry with soft-colored foliage plants. OVERLEAF, FAR RIGHT: This hand-forged Damascus steel Kramer knife is Jamey's pride and joy.

Kale, Corn, and Cherry Tomato Salad

The best of summer in a colorful salad.

Time: 15 minutes
Serves 8

1 pound fresh kale, preferably black Tuscan (lacinato)
6 ears fresh corn
1 cup mixed yellow, red, and orange cherry tomatoes
$3/4$ cup extra virgin olive oil
$1/4$ cup white wine vinegar
$1/2$ teaspoon kosher salt
A few sprinkles freshly ground black pepper

1. Strip off the tough stems of the kale, then slice the leaves in ribbons and cut the ribbons crosswise to make bite-size pieces. (This can also be done in a food processor, but be careful not to overprocess the kale.)

2. Bring a large pot of water to a boil and blanch the ears of corn, then set aside to cool. Using a sharp knife, strip the kernels off the corncobs.

3. Slice the cherry tomatoes in half.

4. Combine the olive oil, vinegar, salt, and pepper in a jar with a lid. Close the lid tightly and shake the jar until the dressing emulsifies.

5. Combine the cut-up kale, corn kernels, and tomato halves in a serving bowl. Pour the dressing on top and stir just enough so that the dressing coats the vegetables. Serve immediately.

COCKTAILS ON THE TERRACE

Dana Cowin is an important name in the food world: For many years editor in chief of *Food & Wine* magazine, she is now chief creative officer of Chefs Club International. With her husband, Barclay Palmer, who is a freelance media producer, they spend their weekends at a late-eighteenth-century former farmhouse in the Hudson Valley. The historic house boasts an original beehive oven, mellow old wide-board pine floors, and a big open kitchen that looks out to a stone terrace and the rolling hills beyond. The terrace was the setting for a fabulous summer cocktail party.

Although Dana knows a great deal about food and cooking, when it comes to giving a party she chooses to outsource. This party's theme was "LIVE eat LOCAL," and accordingly she enlisted a number of local purveyors to supply the elements of the party. Dana found multicolored baby vegetables at Montgomery Place Orchards in Red Hook. The savory Middle Eastern hors d'oeuvres were provided by Serge Madikians, owner-chef of Serevan restaurant in Amenia. From nearby Ancramdale, New York, there were Chaseholm cheeses and Herondale charcuterie. The flowers came from Sol Flower Farm in Millerton, and the cookies from the bakery Back in the Kitchen, in Amenia. A tea cocktail was provided by Connecticut neighbor, resident Sebastian Beckwith, founder of In Pursuit of Tea. Even the whiskey was local: prizewinning bourbon from Hillrock Estate Distillery of Ancram. As the guests—a lively mix of longtime country residents and weekenders—arrived, they were met by music, a mellow mix of jazz and old standards, assembled by cohost, Barclay. From the very first moment, the party sizzled.

OPPOSITE: Big radiant sunflowers decorate a buffet table laden with seasonal delicacies.

TIPS

What makes a great cocktail party?

It starts with the guest list: A good mix of people, some who already know one another and some interesting newcomers. Then the staging: making sure there's room for people to move around, with a well-organized bar area and lots of enticing things to eat and drink. And most important: relaxed hosts, who can enjoy themselves and share the enjoyment with their friends, because all the hard work has been done ahead of time.

Details: For an outdoor party especially, it makes sense to use plastic glasses. Seek out attractive, small disposable plates and forks, so that guests can assemble their own hors d'oeuvres. Have plenty of paper napkins on hand (white is always right), and more than enough ice. Hire helpers, unless you want to spend your party refilling empty glasses and picking up soiled napkins.

OPPOSITE: The front door of this classic eighteenth-century New England farmhouse. CLOCKWISE FROM RIGHT: Dana and her mother, Joyce Cowin. The outdoor buffet, on a table under the kitchen window. Pita bread, falafel, and an array of colorful sauces, with small plates and napkins close at hand. Party guests in bright summer apparel.

OPPOSITE: At the bar, a selection of comestibles.
CLOCKWISE FROM RIGHT: The party's theme: "LIVE eat LOCAL." Dana put together signs identifying the various local sources, with a helpful map. Smoked sausages from Jacüterie, and Bourbon from nearby Hillrock Estate Distillery.

LIVE eat LOCAL ▷

today's specials:

HORS D'OEUVRES — SEREVAN
CHEESE — CHASEHOLM FARM
CHARCUTERIE — JACÜTERIE
TEA PUNCH — IN PURSUIT OF TEA
BOURBON — HILLROCK DISTILLERY
DESSERT — BACK IN THE KITCHEN
FLOWERS — SOL FLOWER FARM

> > > > > < < < < <

Tea-infused Punch with Whiskey and Blueberries

This refreshing punch recipe comes from Sebastian Beckwith of In Pursuit of Tea, importers of fine hand-picked teas from all over the world.

Time: 30 minutes
Makes 20 to 25 cocktails

2 cups fresh blueberries
$\frac{1}{2}$ cup simple syrup, cooled (see Note)
1 cup good bourbon whiskey
$\frac{2}{3}$ cup freshly squeezed lemon juice
2 to 3 cups freshly brewed Darjeeling tea, cooled
$1\frac{1}{2}$ cups sparkling rosé
6 to 8 dashes of Angostura bitters
Superfine sugar
1 lemon, sliced into thin rounds

1. In a shaker or large pitcher, muddle $1\frac{1}{2}$ cups of the blueberries with the simple syrup, mashing the blueberries well. Add the bourbon, lemon juice, and 1 cup ice cubes. Stir thoroughly, then pour the mixture through a fine-mesh strainer set over a punch bowl.

2. Add the tea, the sparkling rosé, and bitters, and stir. Add sugar to taste.

3. Slice the remaining $\frac{1}{2}$ cup blueberries in half and add them to the punch, along with the lemon slices and a large chunk of ice. (You can freeze a big block of ice in a ring mold or plastic container, including blueberries for a nice touch.)

Note: To make the simple syrup: Combine $\frac{1}{2}$ cup water with $\frac{1}{4}$ cup superfine sugar in a small pan and cook over low heat until the sugar is completely dissolved. Bring to a boil and cook for another minute.

Tomato and Watermelon Gazpacho

The success of this unique recipe depends on using equal amounts of tomato and watermelon.

Time: 1 hour, plus 8 hours resting
Serves 20 to 25

2 pounds whole ripe tomatoes, cut into chunks
2 pounds seedless watermelon, peeled and trimmed, cut into chunks
3 red bell peppers, seeded
1 jalapeño or serrano pepper, seeded and sliced
4 garlic cloves, chopped
2 shallots, quartered
$\frac{1}{2}$ white or Spanish onion, sliced
1 to 2 long seedless English cucumbers, peeled and cut into $\frac{1}{2}$-inch slices
Zest of $\frac{1}{2}$ orange, plus 1 whole orange, peeled and separated into segments
1 cup extra virgin olive oil
4 tablespoons sherry or raspberry vinegar
2 teaspoons kosher salt
1 envelope unflavored gelatin, dissolved in $\frac{1}{2}$ cup of water

1. Using a Vitamix blender, puree half of the tomato and watermelon chunks, in batches, until liquefied.

2. Roast the red bell peppers over a flame until lightly charred. When cool, peel the skin and quarter the peppers.

3. In a large nonreactive container, combine the pureed tomato mixture with the rest of the tomatoes and watermelon, the roasted bell pepper, jalapeño, garlic, shallots, onion, cucumber, orange zest, orange segments, and olive oil. Add 1 tablespoon of the vinegar and 1 teaspoon salt and stir. Place the container, covered, in the refrigerator for at least 8 hours. Thirty minutes before serving, remove the container from the refrigerator and process the contents in the blender, in batches, until thoroughly liquefied.

4. Heat $\frac{1}{2}$ cup of the gazpacho with the dissolved gelatin in a small saucepan. When the mixture begins to thicken, add it to the rest of the gazpacho. Add the remaining 3 tablespoons vinegar and 1 teaspoon salt and stir. Serve in small chilled cups.

Falafel

Serge Madikians is the chef of Serevan restaurant, where he serves richly flavored Middle Eastern specialties. Born to an Armenian family, he grew up in Iran and was trained at the French Culinary Institute in New York City. This make-ahead recipe is great party fare: The falafel balls are presented on a buffet, surrounded by the colorful dipping sauces.

Time: 1 to 2 hours preparation, plus
6 to 8 hours refrigeration
Makes 35 to 40 falafel balls

2 cups dried chickpeas, soaked overnight in water to
    cover generously, and drained
1 large onion, cut into eighths
8 garlic cloves, halved
2 jalapeño peppers, stemmed, halved, and seeded
2 teaspoons kosher salt
1½ cups packed fresh flat-leaf parsley, leaves
    and tender stems
1½ cups packed fresh cilantro, leaves and tender stems
1½ teaspoons ground cumin
1½ teaspoons ground coriander
½ teaspoon ground allspice
1½ quarts canola oil for frying
Tahini (recipe follows) and Salad Shirazi (see page 123)
    for serving

1. Spread the drained chickpeas on a rimmed baking sheet and pat dry. Refrigerate, uncovered, for about an hour to dry them out. Working in batches in a food processor, grind the chickpeas until they resemble coarse sand. Transfer to a large bowl.

2. Add the onion, garlic, jalapeños, and salt to the processor and puree. Add the parsley, cilantro, cumin, coriander, and allspice and puree until smooth. Pour this mixture over the ground chickpeas and mix well. Cover and refrigerate the falafel mixture for 6 to 8 hours so the flavors blend. The mixture should be moist but not wet. Using an ice cream scoop or your hands, pack the falafel into 1½-inch balls.

3. In a medium deep skillet, heat the canola oil to 375 F. Fry 6 or 7 falafel balls at a time until golden brown, about 1½ to 2 minutes per batch. Transfer to paper towels to drain. Serve at room temperature with sauces such as tahini and Zhoug, a spicy green sauce, and other condiments. Salad Shirazi is a refreshing accompaniment.

Tahini Sauce

This versatile sauce is great for meat and vegetable dishes.

Time: 10 minutes, plus 1 hour resting
Makes about 1¾ cups

1 cup light tahini (sesame paste), at room temperature
4 garlic cloves, smashed
Juice of 2 lemons, plus more to taste
1½ teaspoons kosher salt, plus more to taste

1. Whisk the tahini in a medium bowl to remove any lumps and stir in the garlic. Combine the lemon juice and ¼ cup water and stir in the salt until dissolved. Combine the lemon water and tahini and whisk until it reaches the consistency of heavy cream. If it is too thick, add a little extra water.

2. Let the tahini stand for at least 1 hour for the flavors to blend. Discard the garlic cloves and season with salt and more lemon juice before serving. If the consistency is still too thick, add more lemon juice and some water.

Note: The tahini sauce can be refrigerated for up to 1 week.

Guests enjoy sampling different taste combinations with Serge's falafel. A plate heaped full of vibrant Mediterranean flavors. CLOCKWISE FROM TOP: Marinated carrots and red cabbage; pickled mango sauce; *ikra* (Armenian-style stewed eggplant); yogurt dip with fresh herbs; falafel; and pita bread. In the center of the plate is hummus.

Eggplant Dip with Labneh and Tahini

The eggplants in this flavorful dip are charred; it's also wonderful with roasted lamb.

Time: 1 hour
Makes 4 cups

3 large firm eggplants
1 cup extra virgin olive oil
1 medium Spanish onion, thickly sliced
6 garlic cloves, chopped
1 tablespoon kosher salt, plus more to taste
1½ cups Greek-style yogurt (labneh)
¾ cup plain tahini paste
   (do not use roasted tahini paste)
2 tablespoons mild vinegar, such as white wine or cider
Juice of 2 lemons, plus more to taste
Juice of 1 lime
Dash of cayenne or Aleppo pepper
½ bunch fresh flat-leaf parsley, chopped
Handful of rose petals for garnish (optional)

1. Preheat the oven to 475°F.

2. Place an ovenproof pan that is big enough to hold the eggplants in the oven to heat.

3. Using a paring knife, score the eggplants' skin in several places. With a long fork, hold the eggplants close to the flame of a gas stove, rotating them so that the skin becomes well charred, about 5 minutes. If you have an electric stove, you can place the eggplants directly on the heating element; otherwise use a grill.

4. Remove the heated pan from the oven and place it over high heat. Add ¼ cup of the olive oil and the sliced onions. Using a wooden spoon, toss the onions in the oil until they begin to brown. Add the garlic and cook, stirring, for another 3 minutes. Add the salt.

5. Place the charred eggplants in the pan on top of the onion-garlic mixture. Pour another ¼ cup olive oil over all, then place the pan in the oven, covered with a lid or aluminum foil. Lower the oven temperature to 375°F and bake for 40 to 45 minutes, or until a sharp knife inserted into the eggplants slides in easily.

6. Remove the pan from the oven and uncover it to cool. Transfer the onion-garlic mixture to a large bowl. Using a sharp knife, cut the eggplants in half. Scoop out the flesh from the skins, add it to the bowl with the onions and garlic, and stir. Discard the eggplant skins.

7. Transfer the eggplant mixture to a food processor and pulse in short spurts until it is evenly blended: Do not overprocess.

8. Transfer the mixture to a medium bowl and add the labneh, tahini, the remaining ½ cup olive oil, the vinegar, lemon juice, lime juice, and cayenne.

9. Let the mixture rest for a couple of hours at room temperature so that the flavors can blend. Stir in the parsley. Taste and adjust for more lemon juice or salt. Garnish with red rose petals, if desired.

10. Serve with pita chips or bread, or as a dipping sauce with falafel.

ABOVE: Serge uses a squeeze bottle to add the tahini sauce to a plateful of spiced beef meatballs on long forks. OPPOSITE: The colorful bowls from Morocco are filled with the artichoke dip, garnished with chopped chives, and the eggplant dip with labneh and tahini, garnished with rose petals. In the background, a plate of crudités.

Artichoke Dip with Chives and Armenian Labneh

This versatile dipping sauce has many uses: It's wonderful with crudités or with pita chips.

Time: 10 minutes, plus 1 hour resting
Serves 6 to 8

4 large artichokes, trimmed to the heart and cooked until tender (you may substitute two 14-ounce canned or jarred artichoke hearts, drained)
½ bunch fresh flat-leaf parsley, finely chopped
1 large shallot, finely diced
Juice of 1 lemon, plus more to taste
1½ cups Armenian or Greek-style yogurt (labneh)
1 tablespoon spicy mustard, such as Russian or Dijon
½ teaspoon salt, plus more to taste
Dash of cayenne pepper
1 bunch fresh chives, very thinly sliced (3 tablespoons)

1. Place the artichoke hearts in a food processor or blender and process to a thick, smooth paste. Add the parsley and shallot and pulse a couple of times to combine.

2. Transfer the artichoke paste to a large bowl. Add the lemon juice, the yogurt, mustard, salt, and cayenne and stir.

3. Put the bowl in the refrigerator for an hour or so to allow the flavors to mingle.

4. Before serving, taste and add more salt or lemon juice as needed. Sprinkle the sliced chives on top.

Salad Shirazi

This refreshing Iranian salad is a perfect side dish for a summertime gathering.

Time: 10 minutes
Makes about 5 cups

1 medium red or white onion, diced (about 1 cup)
2 cups (¼-inch diced), peeled and seeded Persian or European cucumbers
¾ teaspoon kosher salt, plus more to taste
2 cups (¼-inch diced) ripe red tomatoes, drained of excess juice
Juice of ½ lemon
Juice of ½ lime
Cayenne pepper
¼ cup each packed fresh flat-leaf parsley leaves, cilantro leaves, and mint leaves, cut into chiffonade
½ cup extra virgin olive oil

1. Spread the onions in a bowl and top with the cucumbers. Sprinkle evenly with ½ teaspoon of the salt and top with the diced tomatoes. Sprinkle with ¼ teaspoon of the remaining salt and let stand for a few minutes.

2. Sprinkle the lemon juice and lime juice over the salad and add a dash of cayenne. Mix well, then add the herbs and olive oil and toss. Check for seasoning and serve.

OPPOSITE: Dana found these colorful vegetables at a nearby farm stand. Red, yellow, orange, and purple carrots share a plate with purple cabbage and an heirloom variety of cauliflower. RIGHT: Baby red and white onions used for the Salad Shirazi have a sweeter, fresher flavor than the mature version.

Oatmeal Cranberry Cookies

These easy-to-make cookies are always a hit. Both the cookie and blueberry tartlet recipes come from Peggy McEnroe's bakery/restaurant Back in the Kitchen, and are a lovely finale to a party.

Time: 30 minutes
Makes 2 dozen cookies

1 cup sugar
1 cup light brown sugar, packed
2 cups unbleached all-purpose flour
1/2 teaspoon salt
1 teaspoon baking soda
1 teaspoon baking powder
2 cups old-fashioned rolled oats
1/2 cup granola (your favorite)
1 cup dried cranberries
2 large eggs, beaten
8 ounces (2 sticks) unsalted butter, melted,
    plus butter for greasing
1 teaspoon pure vanilla extract

1. Preheat the oven to 350°F.

2. In a large bowl, with a wooden spoon, combine the sugars, flour, salt, baking soda, and baking powder, with the rolled oats, granola, and cranberries.

3. Add the eggs, melted butter, and vanilla and mix thoroughly.

4. Using a 1-ounce cookie scoop, scoop the dough onto a greased 18-inch baking sheet. Bake the cookies for 10 to 15 minutes, until lightly browned.

5. Transfer the cookies to a wire rack and let them cool completely before serving.

An assortment of cookies makes a perfect finale to a cocktail party. From foreground to rear: Oatmeal Cranberry Cookies, Blueberry Johnnycake Crumble Tartlets, and Ginger Cookies.

Blueberry Johnnycake Crumble Tartlets

These blueberry tartlets are topped with johnnycake crumble—johnnycakes are traditional cornmeal breads. The precooked tartlets are filled with blueberry pie filling.

Time: 1 hour
Makes 2 dozen tartlets

1 1/2 cups unbleached all-purpose flour
3/4 cup yellow cornmeal
1/4 cup sugar
1 tablespoon baking powder
1/2 teaspoon baking soda
1/2 teaspoon kosher salt
4 tablespoons (1/2 stick) cold unsalted butter,
    plus more for greasing
1 cup heavy cream, plus more as needed
2 cups blueberry pie filling (your own or store-bought)
1 dozen prebaked tartlet shells (if bought frozen,
    defrost and bake following package directions)

1. Preheat the oven to 400°F.

2. In a large bowl, mix together the flour, cornmeal, the sugars, baking powder, baking soda, and salt with a wooden spoon.

3. Cut the butter into small pieces, then combine with the flour mixture, mixing it with your fingers until it resembles coarse meal.

4. Add the heavy cream and stir with a fork to form a soft, moist dough. If it is dry, add more cream, 1 tablespoon at a time to moisten.

5. In a small saucepan, heat the blueberry pie filling.

6. To assemble the tarts: Spoon the blueberry filling into each of the prebaked tartlets, then top each with a spoonful of the johnnycake crumble dough, and place them on a greased 18-inch baking sheet.

7. Bake the tartlets for 10 to 15 minutes, until the crusts are golden brown. Let them cool completely before serving.

HARVEST GALA

MENU

BEVERAGES
Ginger and Lemongrass Tea
*Autumn Cocktail

STARTER
Chaseholm Cheeses with Honeycomb

MAIN
*Grilled Chicken with Pink Pearl
Apples, Lemon Thyme, and Calvados

SIDES
*Nicole's Roasted Autumn Squash

Roasted Kohlrabi, Pink Turnip,
and Celery Root

DESSERT
*Juniper-flavored Chocolate
Pots de Crème

The Watershed Center occupies a seventy-three-acre former farm outside Millerton, New York. Here guests from a wide variety of progressive disciplines—educational, spiritual, political—hold retreats and attend seminars, while enjoying the center's bucolic amenities. The buildings include a historic farmhouse, a yurt, and several barns. There are hiking trails, a swimmable lake, waterfalls, and streams. It's an environment that nurtures both the body and the spirit.

Food—growing it, cooking it, eating it—is an essential part of the Watershed's mission. The farm features a large organic garden that supplies delicious meals for the staff and guests, as well as providing weekly deliveries of fresh vegetables to local families.

To celebrate the Watershed Center's first full year at the Millerton farm, founding partners Brooke Lehman and Gregg Osofsky hosted a gala dinner for forty. The chef for the event was Nicole LoBue, who is codirector of Kite's Nest, a Hudson, New York–based nonprofit whose educational mission dovetails with Watershed's. Nicole is an acclaimed chef. Her innovative cuisine celebrates seasonal and locally sourced ingredients, some of them harvested in the wild. For the Watershed event she created a dazzling array of tastes and aromas, as exciting to the eye as to the palate.

The tables are set with mix-and-match blue and white linens, with garden flowers in Mason jars, and an assortment of votive candles. OVERLEAF, LEFT: The abundance of the early autumn season; (CLOCKWISE FROM RIGHT) Radicchio and herbs from the garden; braised baby onions; newly picked apples. OVERLEAF, OPPOSITE: Nasturtium flowers are beautiful and edible, with a peppery taste resembling watercress. The jars contain seeds that Nicole LoBue uses in cooking.

TIP

Nicole LoBue uses many foraged ingredients. There's a special thrill to venturing into the wild and finding the first ramps of the spring season, the tiny wild blueberries that grow all over the East Coast, fresh chestnuts and hickory nuts in the fall, and wild catnip to bring home to the family pet. But before you head into the woods, spend some time with an experienced guide. Learn your plants. The best rule is: Never pick or eat anything—berry, mushroom, leaf, flower—unless you know for a fact that it is safe to eat and touch.

The party is about to begin. A jar of late-summer blooms—snapdragons, zinnias, and other old-fashioned favorites—shares table space with artfully arranged cheeses and fruit.

CLOCKWISE FROM RIGHT: The yurt is used for classes and meetings. Nicole, suited up for a big night in the kitchen, in apron, overalls, and sturdy boots. This is the big vegetable garden, with grapevines trained along a fence, and a low range of hills in the background. OPPOSITE: The historic farmhouse, now a thriving center for retreats and workshops.

Autumn Cocktail

This cocktail is made with the berries from autumn olive, or Russian olive (*Elaeagnus umbellate*) trees, which grow wild in woods and fields all over the Northeast. (The silvery-leafed trees, originally planted as ornamentals, are now considered an invasive species.) The edible berries ripen in the fall; they are both tart and sweet, and colored a vibrant fuchsia. Nicole adds locally grown fresh young ginger juice, which is sweeter and more aromatic than the commercial product.

Time: 5 minutes
Makes 1 cocktail

$3\frac{1}{2}$ ounces good rye whiskey
$\frac{1}{2}$ ounce fresh ginger juice
3 tablespoons Autumn Olive Puree (recipe follows)
1 teaspoon freshly squeezed lemon juice
2 dashes of bitters

1. Fill a shaker with chipped ice. Add the whiskey, ginger juice, olive puree, lemon juice, and bitters and shake vigorously for 10 seconds.

2. Strain into a cocktail glass and serve.

OPPOSITE: The finished product, a tangy aperitif.
RIGHT: The autumn olive berries are pureed and then strained.

AUTUMN OLIVE PUREE

Time: 30 minutes
Makes $2\frac{1}{2}$ cups

$1\frac{1}{2}$ cups fresh autumn olive berries (you may substitute $\frac{3}{4}$ cup each raspberries and cherries)
1 teaspoon freshly squeezed lemon juice
$\frac{1}{2}$ to $\frac{3}{4}$ cup raw wildflower honey

1. Put the berries in a blender with $\frac{1}{4}$ cup water, the lemon juice, and honey, and process to a thick puree.

2. Strain the berry puree through a fine-mesh strainer. Store the puree in a glass jar with a lid in the refrigerator for up to a week.

Grilled Chicken with Pink Pearl Apples, Lemon Thyme, and Calvados

This chicken is paired with the pink-fleshed, tart, and complex-flavored antique apple variety called Pink Pearl. If you are unable to find this variety, you may substitute another apple with a similar flavor profile. Here in the Hudson Valley, Pink Pearl apples are available in early autumn at Montgomery Place Orchards, in Red Hook.

Time: 1 hour, plus 6 to 8 hours for brining
Serves 4

Special equipment: wood-burning grill, chimney starter, hardwood charcoal, apple wood chips

One 5-pound roasting chicken cut into 8 pieces, brined for 6 to 8 hours (recipe follows)
3½ tablespoons extra virgin olive oil
1 Meyer lemon, cut into slices, plus 1 lemon, juiced
Pinch of salt
3 to 4 Pink Pearl apples (Idareds or Newtown Pippins may be substituted), peeled, cored, and halved
½ cup Calvados or other apple brandy
4 or 5 fresh lemon thyme branches
Freshly cracked black pepper
Braised shallots (optional)

1. For the grill: Fill a chimney starter with 3 pounds hardwood charcoal and allow it to burn until the coals are evenly lit and glowing. Distribute the coals in an even layer in the bottom of the grill. Place the grill rack as close to the coals as possible.

2. Drain the chicken pieces and discard the brine. Dry the chicken with paper towels. Place in a large bowl, then toss with 3 tablespoons of the olive oil, 2 teaspoons of the lemon juice, and the salt, and set aside.

3. Soak 1 pound apple wood chips in a bucket or large bowl full of cold water for 30 minutes.

4. Toss the apple halves with 1 teaspoon of the remaining lemon juice and the remaining ½ tablespoon olive oil and set aside.

5. Place the chicken, skin side down, in a single layer on the grill rack for about 5 minutes. Turn the pieces over and grill for another 8 minutes. Transfer the chicken pieces to a roasting pan, in a single layer. Set aside.

6. Drain the wood chips. Lift the rack from the grill and push the coals to one side. Place the wood chips on the coals and replace the rack. After about 2 minutes, place the roasting pan with the chicken on the side of the grill where there are no coals or chips. Place the lid on the grill, with the lid's vents slightly open; the vents on the bottom of the grill should stay closed. Smoke the chicken for 10 minutes. It is important to monitor the airflow of the grill: Keeping the lid's vents slightly open allows a nice steady flow of subtle smoke.

7. Check the chicken for doneness and remove from the fire. Let the juices collect in the pan.

8. Add the apple slices to the grill and cook for 5 minutes.

9. Pour the chicken juices into a small saucepan and bring to a simmer over medium heat. Add the Calvados and reduce by half. Add the cooked apple pieces and any remaining lemon juice.

10. Serve the chicken with the apples and juices, lemon thyme, cracked pepper, and braised shallots (if using).

BRINE FOR CHICKEN

Time: 6 to 8 hours
Makes 8 cups (2 quarts)

4 bay leaves, crushed
2 teaspoons juniper berries, crushed
1 tablespoon aniseed
2 medium dried chile peppers
¼ cup kosher salt
Peel of 1 lemon
½ bunch fresh lemon thyme, with leaves and stems

1. Combine the bay leaves, juniper berries, aniseed, and chiles in a mortar and crush with a pestle to release the aromatic oils. Add the salt and mix well.

2. Fill a large pot with 8 cups water. Add the crushed spices to the water, along with the lemon peel and lemon thyme. Mix thoroughly, add the raw chicken, cover, and refrigerate for at least 6 hours.

Nicole's Roasted Autumn Squash

Nicole says, "This is a dish that speaks to a very liminal time here in the Hudson Valley, a favorite moment of mine for the sweet density of earthy squash and the last of the sweet peppers of summer. The fall Concord grapes add a musky note." Kabocha and blue Hubbard are her favorite squashes for this dish, but you could substitute delicata, acorn, or butternut squash. Green coriander seeds—the prize from bolted cilantro—can be crushed in a mortar and with a pestle. They add a delicious sparkle and have many uses: In Sweden coriander turns up in baked breads and sweets, while in India it's a component of curry sauces.

Time: 1 hour
Serves 10

1 kabocha squash (about 2 pounds)
1 blue Hubbard squash (about 2 pounds)
½ cup, plus 1 tablespoon, extra virgin olive oil
1½ tablespoons (depending on taste) kosher salt
8 Jimmy Nardello peppers or other Italian frying peppers
2 tablespoons green coriander seeds (these are the seeds
    that form on cilantro plants after they have bolted;
    dry coriander seeds may be substituted)
1 cup Chile Oil (recipe follows)
2 cups Concord Grape Puree (recipe follows)

1. Preheat the oven to 425°F.

2. Cut each squash in half and clean out the seeds, leaving the edible skins. Cut the halves into wedges and toss with ¼ cup of the olive oil and 1 tablespoon salt. Arrange the squash pieces on parchment paper on rimmed baking sheets, being careful not to crowd them.

3. Toss the Nardello peppers in ¼ cup oil and 1 teaspoon salt and spread on a separate baking sheet.

4. Roast the vegetables for 25 to 35 minutes, checking occasionally for color and a crisp amber caramelization.

5. While the vegetables are roasting, using a mortar and a pestle, pound the green coriander with 1 tablespoon of the oil and ½ teaspoon salt until it is roughly broken down but not pulverized.

6. Combine the roasted squash and peppers on a serving platter. Drizzle the chile oil and the Concord grape puree over all, and sprinkle with the coriander. Serve hot.

LEFT: Cut-up vegetables in roasting pans, ready for the oven.
OPPOSITE, TOP LEFT: The Jimmy Nardello peppers will be tossed with the cooked autumn squash. RIGHT: The Watershed Center's kitchen, with a big restaurant stove and a sturdy work island.

CHILE OIL

This punchy condiment delivers spice and subtle heat. Stir it into dips like guacamole or hummus, or drizzle it on grilled vegetables and meats.

Time: 45 minutes
Makes 2 cups

1½ cups grape seed or other neutral-flavored oil
2 star anise pods
¼ cinnamon stick, preferably cassia cinnamon
1 bay leaf
2 tablespoons Sichuan peppercorns
¾ cup finely chopped dried chile peppers
1 to 1½ teaspoons salt

1. Heat the grape seed oil, star anise, cinnamon stick, bay leaf, Sichuan peppercorns, and chile peppers in a small saucepan over medium-high heat. When the oil starts to bubble slightly, turn the heat down to medium.

2. Let the oil cook for 30 minutes. It should be just barely bubbling. When the oil is done cooking, the seeds and pods should be darker in color, but not blackened. Let the oil cool for 5 minutes.

3. Strain the oil and transfer to a jar with a lid. It will keep in the refrigerator for 1 month.

CONCORD GRAPE PUREE

These big, dark blue grapes are available in markets in the fall; they can often be found in the wild.

Time: 1 hour
Makes 2 cups

1 pound Concord grapes
3 tablespoons freshly squeezed lime juice

1. Pull the grapes from their stems. Place the grapes in a blender and puree them thoroughly. Strain the puree through a fine-mesh strainer, pushing it through with the back of a wooden spoon.

2. Cook the puree in a small saucepan over medium heat until it is reduced by half. Cool to room temperature and then add the lime juice. Store in the refrigerator in a glass jar with a lid for up to 1 week.

Juniper-flavored Chocolate Pots de Crème

These wonderful pots de crème are very easy to prepare, and unless you pour boiling water into the custards, you will be successful. Nicole forages the wild juniper berries in the woods during the fall. Juniper is the secret flavoring in this sublime dessert.

Time: Start at least 6 hours ahead to steep the juniper berries, then 30 minutes preparation and cooking
Serves 8

Special equipment: 8 ovenproof ramekins or custard cups (¾-cup capacity)

3 tablespoons juniper berries (foraged or found on the
     spice shelf in most grocery stores)
2¾ cups heavy cream
8 ounces bittersweet chocolate, coarsely chopped
3 tablespoons sugar
Pinch of salt
8 large egg yolks
Whipped cream and chopped chocolate for serving

1. Lightly crush the juniper berries in a mortar and with a pestle. Steep in the heavy cream for at least 6 hours in the refrigerator (or heat on the stove in a small saucepan on the lowest setting for 4 hours).

2. Preheat the oven to 350°F. Put a large baking pan in the oven and fill it with 2 inches of water. The pan should be big enough to hold the 8 ramekins without their touching one another.

3. In a heatproof bowl set over a saucepan of barely simmering water, melt 7 ounces of chocolate, stirring occasionally. Remove from the heat.

4. Strain the heavy cream through a fine-mesh strainer into a small saucepan to remove the crushed juniper berries.

5. Combine the infused cream, sugar, and salt and bring to a boil. Add the mixture to the melted chocolate and whisk until blended.

6. Place the egg yolks in a medium bowl and whisk. While whisking, add the cream-chocolate mixture in a small stream and continue whisking until blended. Strain the mixture through a fine-mesh strainer into a pitcher with a spout. Pour the mixture into the 8 ramekins.

7. Remove the pan of hot water from the oven and carefully place the ramekins in it. If necessary, add more hot water so that it comes three-quarters of the way up the sides of the ramekins.

8. Return the pan to the oven and bake the pots de crème for 20 minutes, or until the sides are set but the centers jiggle slightly. Remove the pan from the oven and take the ramekins out of the water bath. Let cool and serve warm or chilled with whipped cream and the remaining coarsly chopped chocolate.

LUNCH IN THE ORCHARD

MENU

STARTER
Oysters on the Half Shell with
*Fresh Herb Mignonette

MAIN
*Roasted Cornish Hens with
Fingerling Potatoes

SIDES
*Cider-Braised Brussels Sprouts

*Salad of Baby Spinach Leaves with
Sliced Apples and Calendula Petals

DESSERT
*Pear and Cornmeal Upside-Down
Skillet Cake

Erin French is living proof that a really good cook can make wonderful food anywhere. Proudly self-taught, she is now owner-chef of The Lost Kitchen, a highly acclaimed restaurant in her tiny hometown—population 710—of Freedom, Maine. She grew up helping out in the family's diner. Then, as a young single mother in Belfast, Maine, she launched a series of pop-up dinners in her apartment. Her simple but elegant fare quickly caught on and, with her new husband, she opened a restaurant in Belfast. The restaurant was a success but the marriage failed. In the course of a devastating divorce, Erin lost almost everything: her restaurant, her home, and, very nearly, custody of her child. But she quickly rallied. Moving back to Freedom, she bought a circa 1965 Airstream on craigslist and gutted and decorated it, retrofitting it with vintage appliances. Soon she was driving it about the countryside, seeking out farm-fresh ingredients and cooking pop-up dinners. Customers and favorable press soon followed. Within a year, Erin had found a new venue for her cuisine, in a historic gristmill just down the road from her childhood home. The new Lost Kitchen has won countrywide acclaim; it is booked solid throughout the warm weather months, and Erin has a cookbook in the works.

We caught up with Erin in her Airstream on a sunny fall day when she was cooking lunch in the orchard at Dorolenna Farm, an organic farm that sources many of the ingredients Erin uses at the restaurant. Farm owner Victoria Marshall—who also waits tables at The Lost Kitchen—was there, picking pears and herbs for our meal, which was served on Victoria's family china. The tiny trailer kitchen filled with intoxicating aromas. Erin deftly chopped and sliced, slipping her prized cast-iron pans in and out of the tiny oven. As she worked, she discussed her cooking philosophy: No hard-and-fast rules, just simple, honest food using the best ingredients, which are always recognizable on the plate.

A sunny autumn day in Maine, in an orchard full of ripening fruit. A sheepskin from a nearby farm softens the seat at the head of the table. OVERLEAF, CLOCKWISE FROM TOP LEFT: The table is set with heirloom china on top of slate "place mats," on a rustic picnic table. The 1965 Airstream was found on craigslist. Erin turned it into a cozy traveling home and a venue for pop-up dinner parties. Erin and Victoria gather slate pieces for the table.

GAME PLAN

With just one small oven, a two-burner cooktop, and a miniscule sink, Erin served a simple but very sophisticated feast. Here's how: Start the Cornish hens first, allowing 2 hours before the time you plan to sit down at the table. While the hens cook in the oven, prepare the pear dessert through step 5. Prep the Brussels sprouts and put together a light salad, before serving the hors d'ouevre. (Erin served oysters on the half shell.) Clean up as you work. (Guests will offer to help.) When the hens come out of the oven, turn the temperature down to 350°F to finish the Brussels sprouts. Complete the pear cake and let it cook in the oven while the guests enjoy the main course.

Fresh Herb Mignonette

Erin gets fresh oysters delivered from the Maine coast; she arranges them on a bed of seaweed and shaved ice and spoons her mignonette sauce on top of each oyster. The herbs in this sauce were picked just minutes ahead of time.

Time: 5 minutes
Makes ½ cup (enough for 12 oysters)

¼ cup rice wine vinegar
2 tablespoons finely chopped shallots
1 teaspoon finely chopped fresh chives
1 teaspoon finely chopped fresh dill
¼ teaspoon freshly ground black pepper

Mix the rice wine vinegar, shallots, chives, dill, and pepper in a small bowl. Serve over freshly shucked oysters on the half shell.

ABOVE: The wood-handled knife at top is a special oyster knife. Opening these delectable bivalves requires skill and strength. OPPOSITE: The oysters, dressed with mignonette sauce, are presented on a bed of fresh seaweed.

Fingerling potatoes, onions, and fennel, fresh from the garden. OPPOSITE: The Cornish hens, cooked together with the little potatoes and decorated with edible flowers, come to the table on an antique platter.

Roasted Cornish Hens with Fingerling Potatoes

This satisfying one-pot meal works for either lunch or dinner. The juices from the well-seasoned hens make a perfect marriage with the tiny potatoes.

Time: 1½ hours
Serves 4

Four 1½-pound Cornish hens
½ cup fresh lavender flowers (optional)
½ cup fresh or dried sage leaves
1 lemon, quartered
1 whole head garlic, quartered
Sea salt and freshly ground black pepper
2 large white onions, thinly sliced
1 pound fingerling potatoes, unpeeled
2 tablespoons good olive oil
4 tablespoons (½ stick) unsalted butter, melted
Nasturtium flowers for garnish (optional)

1. Preheat the oven to 425°F.

2. Pat the hens dry and stuff each one with one-quarter of the herbs, one-quarter of the lemon, one-quarter of the garlic, and a good pinch of salt and pepper. Truss the hens: Twist the wing tips upward and inward behind the shoulder and fold against the back of the bird. With a small paring knife, make a ½-inch slit just above the base of the backbone. Take each leg and pull the tip of the bone through the slit.

3. Spread the sliced onions and the potatoes in the bottom of a 12-inch cast-iron pan, then toss them with salt, pepper, and the olive oil.

4. Place the stuffed hens on top of the vegetables in the pan, leaving space between the hens so they will brown well.

5. Brush the hens with melted butter and rub more salt and pepper on the skin.

6. Roast the hens in the preheated oven for about an hour, until the juices run clear and an instant-read thermometer inserted into the thickest part of a thigh reads 165°F. Serve the hens over the potatoes and onions. Garnish with nasturtium (if using).

Cider-Braised Brussels Sprouts

Apple cider and shallots enrich this hearty autumn
vegetable. Quickly cooked with butter, shallots, and
apple cider, the sprouts are tender and delicious.

Time: 30 minutes
Serves 4

1 pound Brussels sprouts
2 tablespoons good olive oil
½ cup finely chopped shallots
Kosher salt and freshly ground black pepper
¼ cup apple cider
2 tablespoons unsalted butter

1. Preheat the oven to 350°F.

2. Trim the Brussels sprouts: Remove the tough outer
leaves and stem, and cut each Brussels sprout in half.

3. Heat a 10-inch cast-iron pan on medium heat. Add
the olive oil and shallots. Cook over medium heat until
the shallots turn translucent.

4. Add the trimmed Brussels sprouts. Cook for
1 minute, tossing frequently. Season with salt and
pepper, then add the apple cider. Reduce the cider
for 1 minute, then add the butter.

5. Put the pan in the oven and cook until the Brussels
sprouts are tender but still a bit crunchy, about 3
minutes. Serve hot.

Salad of Baby Spinach Leaves with Sliced Apples and Calendula Petals

This pretty salad rounds out the feast. The fresh young
onions were picked earlier in the day.

Time: 30 minutes
Serves 6

1 tablespoon finely chopped sweet onion
3 tablespoons rice wine vinegar
¼ cup extra virgin olive oil
¼ teaspoon freshly ground black pepper
1 pound whole baby spinach leaves, washed and dried
1 crisp apple, cored and very thinly sliced (do not peel)
¼ cup calendula petals for sprinkling
    (or substitute nasturtium petals)

1. Combine the chopped onion and rice wine vinegar
in a small bowl and macerate for 10 minutes. Add the
olive oil and pepper and whisk to combine.

2. Put the spinach leaves and apple slices in a serving bowl.

3. Pour the vinaigrette over the spinach and apple slices, toss
gently, then sprinkle the calendula petals on top and serve.

ABOVE: A basket of just-picked apples and vegetables.

Pear and Cornmeal Upside-Down Skillet Cake

This favorite family recipe was passed down from Erin's grandmother. The pears came from the orchard, where we had lunch, and were picked the morning she prepared the cake.

Time: 1 hour
Serves 8

4 firm but ripe pears (Bosc or Bartlett)
12 tablespoons (1½ sticks) unsalted butter, at room temperature
1½ cups granulated sugar
1 cup unbleached all-purpose flour
½ cup yellow cornmeal
1½ teaspoons baking powder
½ teaspoon salt
2 large eggs
1 teaspoon pure vanilla extract
½ cup sour cream
Confectioners' sugar

1. Preheat the oven to 350°F.

2. Prepare the pears: Stem, peel, halve, and core the pears, using a melon baller to scoop out the cores. Without cutting through the top ½ inch of the pear halves, slice each one lengthwise, 4 or 5 times, keeping the stem ends intact.

3. Heat 4 tablespoons (½ stick) of the butter in a 10-inch well-seasoned cast-iron pan over medium heat. When the butter has melted, add ½ cup of the granulated sugar and stir.

4. Arrange the partially sliced pear halves decoratively in a concentric circle in the pan, rounded side down. Caramelize the pears over medium heat until the sugar has turned a deep golden color, 15 to 20 minutes.

5. Make the batter (you can do this while the pears are cooking): Combine the flour, cornmeal, baking powder, and salt in a small bowl and set aside. In a separate bowl, with a whisk, beat the remaining 8 tablespoons (1 stick) butter until soft, slowly adding the remaining 1 cup granulated sugar. Beat until light and fluffy. Add the eggs, one at a time, beating until they are well combined. Add the vanilla and sour cream. Stir in the flour mixture. (This can all be done a few hours ahead of time.)

6. Pour the batter over the cooked pears and bake in the skillet in the oven for about 25 minutes, until a tester inserted into the cake comes out clean.

7. Let the cake cool on a rack for about 5 minutes, then run a knife around the edge of the pan and invert the cake onto a serving plate. Dust with confectioners' sugar and serve warm.

TIPS

Like many serious cooks, Erin treasures her sturdy cast-iron pans. Nothing beats them for even cooking and heat retention. They are inexpensive to buy and will last forever if treated kindly.

New pans need to be "seasoned": Coat the surface with vegetable oil and heat the pan in a 300°F oven for an hour or so, then wipe the pan dry. Clean your pan after each use with hot water and a sponge or a soft brush. A little kosher salt will help to remove stubborn grime; do not use soap as it will strip away the pan's seasoning. Always dry the pan thoroughly. If the surface looks dull, rub a bit of oil into it. If the pan becomes rough or rusted, re-season it in the oven.

FIRESIDE DINING

MENU

STARTERS
Cheese Plate with Sliced Pears
*Hearty Vegetable Soup

MAIN
*Fireplace Grilled Lamb Chops

SIDES
*Steamed or Roasted
Fresh Organic Vegetables

*Salad of Spicy Greens

DESSERT
*Berry Cobbler

The Marston House, in Wiscasset, Maine, is a favorite destination for antiquers, collectors, and design aficionados. The shop—an Aladdin's cave of lovingly curated collections of old textiles, eighteenth- and nineteenth-century furniture, vintage kitchenware, European and American folk art, and much more— is open from May to the end of September. Proprietors Sharon and Paul Mrozinski spend the rest of the year based in their home in the South of France, traveling about Europe as they restock the store for the coming season. They buy only things that they are emotionally drawn to, and they are glad to pass them on to the next owner. The shop at The Marston House has so much charm that it makes one want to move right in. Happily for visitors, there are two lovingly furnished bed and breakfast rooms available in an adjacent carriage house.

For Sharon and Paul, life and work are a seamless continuum. In Maine and in France they cook every day, buying fresh organic produce from local markets. The food is wholesome and delicious; they bring their aesthetic passion to the kitchen and the table. When they first moved into The Marston House, some twenty years ago, the house, which dates to the late eighteenth century, needed months of renovation work. Lacking a proper kitchen, they learned to cook in the big fireplace in their dining room, and they still enjoy this primal process almost every day.

Paul and Sharon cook many of their meals in this fireplace, in the living room of their historic home. On the stone mantel, between the bird portraits, a collection of birds' eggs under an antique glass dome.

ABOVE AND OPPOSITE PAGE: To accompany the pre-dinner wine: a selection of cheeses with crisp little Seckel pears. This tasty fruit is one of the pleasures of the autumn season. RIGHT: The iron kettle hangs on a hook inside the fireplace. Within, vegetables slowly roast as the grill heats up.

CLOCKWISE FROM TOP LEFT: You can never have too many wooden serving boards and baskets. The kitchen stove, with rice cooking. Paul pours a glass of wine, as Sharon arranges cooked vegetables in a big ceramic bowl. OPPOSITE: Sharon's pear collection: On the shelves, pears in wood, ceramic, and stone, displayed alongside prints and paintings and photographs of her favorite fruit. On the left, the prize of the group—a huge ceramic pear sculpture.

CLOCKWISE FROM TOP LEFT: An early blue-painted Maine cupboard provides storage for everyday dishes and cutlery. Hydrangeas from the garden of The Marston House's next-door b&b. The staghorn-handled knife and fork are English; the spoon comes from a set of reproduction Tudor flatware. OPPOSITE: The dinner table. In the fore-ground, a plate of roasted vegetables—baby carrots, leeks, fingerling potatoes; in the background, the grilled lamb chops. The two small blue bowls contain a compote of cherry tomatoes to serve with the lamb.

Hearty Vegetable Soup

Paul and Sharon enjoy this tasty, healthful soup every morning; they often serve it as a first course for lunch or dinner. The ingredients vary according to the season. The soup can be made ahead and stored for several days in the refrigerator.

Time: 20 minutes
Serves 4 to 6

5 medium carrots
1 small head red cabbage
4 celery stalks, with tops
1 cup kale
1 cup Swiss chard
5 garlic cloves, minced
One 1-inch chunk fresh ginger, minced
1 teaspoon raw turmeric root, minced (or 1 teaspoon dried)
1 teaspoon miso
2 cups cooked rice, preferably a mixture of brown rice, wild rice, and forbidden rice

1. Chop the carrots, cabbage, celery, kale, and chard into bite-size pieces.

2. Put the vegetable pieces in a large stockpot with 5 cups water. Add the garlic, ginger, and turmeric. Bring to a boil, uncovered, then turn the heat down to a slow simmer. Cook for 20 minutes.

3. Spoon some of the vegetable broth into each bowl and stir in the miso.

4. Add the cooked vegetables and serve over rice.

Sharon and Paul always start their day with this hearty stew of seasonal produce. They follow a healthy diet, including lots of fresh organic vegetables, which they buy from farm stands and local markets. ABOVE, RIGHT: Cooked rice in a terra-cotta dish from Blue Hill, Maine. OPPOSITE: Soup is served.

Fireplace Grilled Lamb Chops

Paul and Sharon use a Tuscan grill, a metal rack with legs that sits above the fire, to grill meat. The fire is made with aged hardwoods (mainly oak with some apple trimmings), and lighter fluid is never used because it adds a bad taste, besides being toxic.

Time: 1 hour
Serves 4

Four 1-inch-thick loin lamb chops, at room temperature
1 teaspoon Maldon sea salt flakes
½ cup dried thyme branches

1. Make a fire in the fireplace or grill. The fire will be ready when the flames have died down and the coals are still very hot. Paul tests it by holding his hand above the coals: They are ready when he can't leave his hand for more than a few seconds.

2. Season the chops with salt, then lay them on a bed of thyme branches on the grill's metal rack.

3. Place the rack 4 inches above the coals. Cook the chops for 4 minutes on each side and serve at once.

LEFT: The lamb chops are on the grill. A plate with serving tools sits close at hand on an antique trivet. OPPOSITE, LEFT TO RIGHT: A terra-cotta bowl of onions, garlic, and shallots sits close to the stove, ready for use. Fingerling potatoes and baby leeks in a ceramic bowl, ready to go into the oven.

Steamed or Roasted Fresh Organic Vegetables

Slow cooking brings out the vegetables' flavors. Paul and Sharon have an iron cauldron that swings above the hot coals in their fireplace. Vegetables cooked with this method develop a rich, smoky taste. This recipe also works well in a conventional oven.

Time: 1 hour
Serves 4

$^1\!/_4$ to $^1\!/_2$ pound each young fresh carrots, leeks, Brussels sprouts, and fingerling potatoes
$^1\!/_4$ cup garlic cloves, unpeeled
$^1\!/_4$ cup medium shallots, unpeeled
Maldon sea salt flakes
2 tablespoons extra virgin olive oil

1. Preheat the oven to 375 F, or heat an iron cauldron over a hot fire.

2. Prepare the vegetables: Trim the carrots, leaving them long. Wash the leeks very well and trim off the tough outer leaves. Remove the outer leaves and the tough stems from the Brussels sprouts. Wash the potatoes but leave the skins on.

3. Dry the vegetables thoroughly. Arrange them in a roasting pan, uncovered, leaving space between the vegetables so they do not touch. (You may need more than one pan.) Add the garlic and shallots to each pan. If using the iron cauldron method, arrange the vegetables and cover the cauldron tightly with a lid or aluminum foil. Let the vegetables steam over the fire.

4. Sprinkle the vegetables with sea salt and the olive oil. Cook until tender, about 45 minutes. The carrots will take the longest.

Salad of Spicy Greens

This tasty salad is a year-round staple in Sharon and Paul's kitchen. It may include herbs or edible flowers or whatever is available at the farmers' market or foraged.

Time: 10 minutes
Serves 6 to 8

Juice of ½ lemon
2 tablespoons extra virgin olive oil
1 or 2 large garlic cloves, finely chopped
1 head young broccoli, chopped into small pieces,
    tough stem removed
2 to 3 cups mixed fresh salad greens, such as arugula,
    mizuna, cilantro, and mustard greens
Edible flowers for garnish (optional)

1. Make the dressing: In a large glass or wooden bowl, combine the lemon juice and olive oil, mixing with a fork until emulsified. Stir in the chopped garlic and broccoli. Set aside but do not refrigerate.

2. Put the greens into a salad spinner filled with cold water. Rinse the greens, then pour off the water and spin until dry.

3. Toss the greens thoroughly in the bowl with the dressing. Add edible flowers, if using, and serve immediately.

Berry Cobbler

This simple dessert celebrates the rich flavor of summer berries. It's wonderful with a dollop of lightly whipped cream.

Time: 1 hour
Serves 6 to 8

1½ cups fresh blueberries, preferably wild
    Maine blueberries
1½ cups fresh raspberries
½ cup sugar
1 tablespoon cornstarch
1 cup freshly squeezed orange juice (or apple cider)
1 cup unbleached all-purpose flour
1½ teaspoons baking powder
½ teaspoon salt
3 tablespoons unsalted butter, at room temperature
½ cup whole milk
Lightly whipped cream for serving

1. Preheat the oven to 400°F.

2. Wash the blueberries and raspberries and remove any stems or leaves.

3. Combine the sugar, cornstarch, and orange juice in a small saucepan. Bring just to a boil, then add the berries and stir gently.

4. Pour the mixture into a 1½-quart baking dish and set aside.

5. Make the crumble: Combine the flour, baking powder, salt, and butter in a small bowl. Blend together with a fork until it resembles a coarse meal. Stir in the milk.

6. Drop the crumble by spoonfuls over the hot berry mixture. Bake for 30 minutes.

7. Serve warm or at room temperature, with a dollop of whipped cream.

THE FAMILY FEAST

—Abby Adams

MENU

BEVERAGE

*Thanxmas Cocktail

*Gravlax

*Classic Mignonette Sauce for
Oysters on the Half Shell

MAINS

*Patrick Adams's Cuban Roast Pork
with Mojo Sauce

Roasted Turkey Breast

SIDES

*Miniature Corn Muffins

Scalloped Potatoes

Brussels Sprouts

*Mashed Sweet Potatoes
with Chipotles

Kale Salad

DESSERTS

*Adrienne's Pear Almond Tart

*Melissa's Cranberry Tart
with Nut Crust

Pumpkin Pie

Instead of Thanksgiving and/or Christmas, my combined Adams-Westlake family celebrates Thanxmas. It takes place on a Saturday afternoon midway between the two holidays. Like Thanksgiving it's a feast, with a roomful of people of all ages (twenty-seven this year), eating masses of good food. Like Christmas there are presents, carol singing, and decorations. Like Thanksgiving it's all over in a day. And since it's not a public holiday, the travel is not a big hassle.

The Adamses are a foodie clan. My son, Patrick Adams, is a professional chef; my daughter, Adrienne, is a caterer. They each do as much cooking in their free time as on the job. The rest of us, and the Westlakes, range from talented home cooks to helpful sous-chefs and dishwashers. When we all get together, the kitchen explodes with food. The centerpiece on the Thanxmas menu is a Cuban recipe for roast pork that has become a tradition in our family. (For the non-pork eaters, I roast a turkey breast.) I buy the meat—an organic, locally grown pork shoulder, ten pounds or more—several days ahead of time and marinate it in the refrigerator. On Saturday it will cook all day, emerging at dinnertime succulent and flavorful. While the pork is marinating, I'll make gravlax: fresh salmon cured in salt, sugar, and dill. As my everyday dinner table seats just ten, at Thankxmas I enlist three folding tables that I dress up with white tablecloths, red cotton napkins, candles, and greenery from outdoors. This is the nonhectic part of the preparation.

Thanxmas day, 2:00 p.m.: Guests start arriving, bearing gifts, dishes to be reheated in the oven, desserts. I gently herd the noncooks into the living room, where there are drinks and sparkling cider. The gravlax comes out of the refrigerator; Patrick arrives with a bucket of fresh oysters from Long Island. Around four o'clock we all sit down at the table. Besides pork and turkey, there are side dishes: Brussels sprouts, scalloped potatoes, mashed sweet potatoes, miniature corn muffins, and kale salad, all contributed by guests. I'm a firm believer in outsourcing.

An hour or so later, well fed, we return to the living room for dessert. Coffee is served, presents opened; we decorate the tree, sing carols, take turns at washing dishes. Happy Thanxmas to all, and to all a good night.

The house gets dressed up for the season. CLOCKWISE, FROM TOP LEFT: The kitchen door with a lighted holiday wreath. This upright piano dates from 1908; it came with the house. Lighting the candles in the living room. OPPOSITE: The plate rack is French; it holds an eclectic collection of mostly white ironstone china. PREVIOUS PAGE: Place cards are a must for large family gatherings. Joan Osofsky styled these for me: Handwritten paper tags are tied to the red napkins with green velvet ribbons.

TIPS

Having restaurant-trained
people in the family is a boon.
At serving time, we arrange
all the food on the kitchen
island. Guests bring their
plates in and my helpers and
I dish up the meal.

I give three or four big
parties every year. Folding
tables and chairs for these
occasions are stored in the
barn. It makes sense to buy
these rather than rent them.

I have two dishwashers. Most
days I use just the little one,
but when I'm entertaining,
I keep them both running,
in rotation. The kitchen
stays tidy and usable.

Can you have too many candlesticks? I don't think
so. The drawing, by my mother, Persis Washburn,
depicts a lazy winter afternoon in the Maine
farmhouse where she grew up. I decked the house
with evergreen branches from the property.

Thanxmas Cocktail

This cocktail—besides being pretty to look at—is refreshing and festive. The proportions can be tweaked to make a lighter drink.

Time: 5 minutes
Makes 1 cocktail

2 ounces vodka
2 ounces Campari
2 ounces Sanpellegrino–brand Pompelmo
   (or another good-quality grapefruit soda)
1 thin orange slice

Combine the vodka, Campari, and Pompelmo in a tall glass filled with plenty of ice cubes. Garnish with the orange slice.

OPPOSITE: Beverages, pitchers, and glassware, in an antique Canadian hutch in the kitchen.
ABOVE: A colorful aperitif begins the festivities.

Gravlax

This is a Scandinavian recipe for cured salmon; instead of being smoked, the fish marinates for a day or two in the refrigerator. The salmon has a nice firm texture, and makes a great party dish.

Time: 15 minutes preparation, plus 24 to 48 hours in the refrigerator
Serves 12 to 20

One 2- to 3-pound whole skin-on fillet of salmon
1 cup kosher salt
2 cups sugar
1 bunch coarsely chopped fresh dill
Thin slices black or pumpernickel bread
Gravlax Sauce (recipe follows)
Lemon wedges for garnish (optional)

1. Go over the salmon with tweezers to remove any small bones. Place the fillet, skin side down, on a tray on several layers of overlapping plastic wrap.

2. Mix the salt, sugar, and half of the dill (reserve the remaining chopped dill in the refrigerator for serving) and use the mixture to cover the fillet, coating it thickly.

3. Wrap plastic wrap tightly around the fish and put the fish in the refrigerator for 1 to 2 days.

4. Unwrap the fillet and rinse off the salt mixture. Dry well.

5. To serve: Slice the salmon off the skin, very thinly, and arrange on thin slices of black or pumpernickel bread. Garnish with the remaining dill, a dollop of gravlax sauce, and lemon wedges (if using).

Note: Gravlax will keep in the refrigerator for up to 5 days.

GRAVLAX SAUCE

Time: 5 minutes
Makes 2 cups

1 cup finely chopped fresh dill
Juice of ½ lemon
1 tablespoon red wine vinegar
1 tablespoon honey
1 teaspoon chopped shallot
¼ cup mayonnaise
1 tablespoon Dijon mustard
¼ cup extra virgin olive oil
¼ cup neutral oil, such as safflower or canola
Kosher salt and freshly ground black pepper

1. Combine the dill, lemon juice, vinegar, honey, shallot, mayonnaise, and mustard in a blender or food processor.

2. Process on high speed until smooth, then reduce the speed and slowly add the olive oil and neutral oil until they are absorbed. Season with salt and pepper.

RIGHT: The gravlax as it comes out of the refrigerator after marinating. The plastic wrap will be discarded, the salt rinsed off, and the gravlax will be sliced. OPPOSITE: The sliced gravlax, plated, sauced, and garnished.

Classic Mignonette Sauce for Oysters on the Half Shell

I am fortunate to have three skilled oyster shuckers in my family. However, it's possible to buy freshly shucked oysters from a good fish market; keep the oysters on ice and serve within twenty-four hours.

Time: 5 minutes
Makes 1 cup (enough for 24 oysters)

1 cup red wine vinegar
1 shallot, finely chopped
½ teaspoon freshly ground black pepper

Stir the vinegar, shallot, and pepper in a small bowl. Serve with freshly shucked oysters, arranged on a platter with plenty of ice. (We used snow.)

Patrick Adams's Cuban Roast Pork with Mojo Sauce

This festive recipe is a family tradition; it's easy to cook because all the work is done in advance. Pork shoulder is the tastiest, juiciest cut. I buy the meat from a local organic farm.

Time: 1 hour preparation, plus 24 to 36 hours in the refrigerator and 6 to 7 hours cooking
Serves 20

One 10-pound (or two 5-pound) whole bone-in pork shoulder roast(s)
1 head garlic, cloves separated and peeled
1 teaspoon dried cumin
2 tablespoons dried oregano
2 tablespoons kosher salt, plus more for sprinkling over the marinated meat
1 cup freshly squeezed lime juice
½ cup freshly squeezed orange juice
2 tablespoons olive oil
1 tablespoon freshly ground black pepper, plus more for sprinkling over the marinated meat
Mojo Sauce (recipe follows)

1. Place the meat in a large bowl and, using a sharp knife, stab all over, twisting the knife to make holes half the depth of the meat.

2. Place the garlic, cumin, oregano, salt, lime juice, orange juice, olive oil, and pepper in a blender or food processor, and process until the garlic is finely chopped.

3. Rub the mixture all over the meat, forcing it into the holes.

4. Cover the meat tightly with plastic wrap and refrigerate for a day or two, turning it occasionally.

5. On the morning of the party, preheat the oven to 350°F.

6. Remove the pork from the refrigerator, discarding the plastic wrap and marinade. Sprinkle the meat all over with salt and pepper and transfer it to a roasting pan.

7. Cook the meat for 30 minutes, then reduce the oven temperature to 275 F.

8. After 2 hours, add water to the pan if the juices are beginning to blacken.

A loose tent of aluminum foil can be used to keep the meat from getting too brown. The roast is done when the juices run clear and the internal temperature reaches 190 F; this may take 6 to 7 hours. Once done, the meat can rest for as long as an hour. Reserve the juices in the pan for the Mojo Sauce.

9. Carve the roast into thick slices and serve with mojo sauce on the side.

MOJO SAUCE

Time: 15 minutes
Makes 3 cups

1 cup juices from the pork roasting pan
6 garlic cloves, finely chopped
1 cup extra virgin olive oil
2 teaspoons ground cumin
1 cup freshly squeezed lime juice
$^1\!4$ cup freshly squeezed orange juice
1 cup coarsely chopped fresh cilantro
Kosher salt and freshly ground black pepper

1. Deglaze the pan juices: Add $^1\!2$ cup water to the juices in the roasting pan, bring to a simmer, and stir with a wooden spoon for 3 minutes.

2. In a small saucepan, sweat the garlic in the olive oil over low heat for 3 minutes, just until it turns translucent.

3. Strain 1 cup of the reduced pan juices into the pan with the garlic. Add the cumin. Cool to room temperature.

4. Stir in the lime juice, orange juice, and cilantro. Season with salt and pepper.

Miniature Corn Muffins

These little treats are always popular. I put them on the table just before the main course comes out.

Time: 1 hour
Makes 48 miniature muffins

2 cups unbleached all-purpose flour
1½ cups yellow cornmeal
2 tablespoons baking powder
1 teaspoon salt
2 teaspoons crushed red pepper flakes
1 tablespoon dried cumin
1 cup sour cream
1 cup whole milk yogurt
1¼ cups 2 percent milk
4 tablespoons (½ stick) unsalted butter, melted
2 large eggs, at room temperature, beaten
¾ cup diced scallions
1½ cups canned creamed corn
¼ cup finely diced jalapeño pepper (optional)
2 cups grated Cheddar cheese

1. Preheat the oven to 375°F.

2. Sift together the flour, cornmeal, baking powder, and salt into a large bowl. Stir in the red pepper flakes and cumin.

3. In another bowl, combine the sour cream, yogurt, and milk, and mix well. Add the melted butter and eggs, and stir to combine.

4. Add the sour cream mixture to the flour mixture and mix gently. Add the scallions, creamed corn, jalapeños (if using), and cheese, and stir to combine.

5. Grease four mini muffin tins with cooking oil spray. Spoon the batter into the tins and bake for about 25 minutes, until a toothpick inserted into the muffins comes out clean.

Note: The leftover muffins can be reheated.

Mashed Sweet Potatoes with Chipotles

This side dish strikes a nice balance between sweet and spicy. It can be prepared the day before and reheated 30 minutes before serving.

Time: 2 hours
Serves 12 to 16

8 large yellow sweet potatoes (about 4 pounds)
4 tablespoons (½ stick) unsalted butter, softened, plus 1 tablespoon to grease the baking dish
½ cup maple syrup
2 teaspoons adobo sauce from canned chipotles
Kosher salt and freshly ground black pepper

1. Preheat the oven to 350°F.

2. Place the whole sweet potatoes on a rimmed baking sheet and sprinkle with 1 cup water. Bake for 45 minutes to 1 hour, until very soft inside. Remove from the oven and let cool.

3. Scrape the flesh out of the skins and discard the peels. In a large bowl, mash the potato flesh with the butter, maple syrup, and adobo sauce. Season with salt and pepper. (This step can be done up to 1 day ahead; refrigerate until ready to bake.)

4. Heat the oven to 400°F. Scoop the potato mixture into a greased 9 by 12-inch baking dish. Heat until bubbly. Transfer to an attractive bowl and serve hot.

Adrienne's Pear Almond Tart

My daughter, Adrienne Adams, loves to bake. This elegant tart is one of her specialties. The pastry dough can be made one or two days ahead. The pie can be finished the morning of the event and served at room temperature.

Time: For the pastry dough, 10 minutes, plus 1 hour resting. For finishing the tart, 1½ hours
Serves 10

For the pastry dough
1¼ cups unbleached all-purpose flour,
    plus more for dusting
¾ cup almond meal
½ teaspoon salt
1 tablespoon sugar
8 tablespoons (1 stick) unsalted butter, cold,
    cut into small pieces

1. In a food processor, pulse the flour, almond meal, salt, and sugar together. Add the butter pieces and pulse until the crumbs are no larger than peas. Add 2 tablespoons ice water and pulse 3 or 4 times. If the dough doesn't hold together when pressed between your fingers, add more ice water a spoonful at a time until the dough sticks.

2. Shape the dough into a thick disk, wrap it in plastic wrap, and chill until firm, about 1 hour. The dough can be made up to 2 days ahead.

For finishing the tart
3 ripe but firm Bosc pears
10 tablespoons (1¼ sticks) unsalted
    butter, softened
¾ cup sugar
2 large eggs
1 teaspoon pure vanilla extract
½ teaspoon pure almond extract
¼ cup unbleached all-purpose flour
2 tablespoons confectioners' sugar

1. Preheat the oven to 350 F.

2. To caramelize the pears: Peel, halve, and core the pears. Melt 4 tablespoons of the butter in a saucepan over medium heat. Stir in ¼ cup of the sugar. When the sugar melts, add the pears, rounded side up, and cook until lightly browned. Turn the pears to cook on the other side. Remove the pears and set aside.

3. To make the filling: In the bowl of a stand mixer with paddle, beat together the remaining ½ cup sugar and 6 tablespoons butter until pale and fluffy. Add the eggs, one at a time, beating well after each addition, then add the vanilla and almond extract. Add the flour and mix until just combined.

4. To finish the pastry: Dust a rolling pin with flour. Place the refrigerated dough on lightly floured parchment paper. Working quickly, and turning the dough frequently, roll out the dough to a 12-inch round. Use the parchment paper to place the dough on a 9-inch tart pan with a removable bottom. Carefully press the dough onto the sides of the pan, then use a sharp knife to trim off any excess dough from the rim.

5. To assemble the tart: Spread the filling in the tart shell. Cut the pear halves across into 6 slices. Holding the slices together, fan them out in a decorative pattern.

6. Bake the tart for 30 to 40 minutes, until the filling is lightly puffed and firm. Dust with confectioners' sugar before serving.

OPPOSITE: The dessert table is set up at one end of the living room, with pies, whipped cream, serving utensils, and demitasse cups. The branches in the big earthenware jug come from an ornamental pear tree in my backyard. I pick the red leaves in October and they hold their color for months.

Melissa's Cranberry Tart with Nut Crust

This gorgeous dessert is the perfect ending for a holiday meal: The tartness of the cranberries is a welcome contrast to the rich foods that precede it. Melissa Sorman's recipe is adapted from one called Cranberry Nut Tart, in *Entertaining* by Martha Stewart.

Time: 2 hours
Serves 10

For the crust
½ cup toasted nuts, such as walnuts and/or almonds
8 tablespoons (1 stick) unsalted butter, at room temperature, plus 1 teaspoon for greasing the pan
2 tablespoons sugar
1½ cups unbleached all-purpose flour
1 large egg, beaten
½ teaspoon pure almond (or vanilla) extract

1. In a food processor, process the nuts to an even cornmeal consistency. Add the butter, sugar, flour, egg, and almond extract, and process well.

2. Press the mixture into a 9-inch buttered springform pan and place it in the refrigerator to chill for 30 minutes.

3. While the crust is chilling, reheat the oven to 350°F.

4. Bake the crust for 18 to 20 minutes, until golden brown. Set aside to cool.

For the filling
3 cups (one 12-ounce package) fresh cranberries
1½ cups sugar
½ cup red currant jelly (or raspberry or strawberry jam)
1 envelope unflavored gelatin, softened in ¼ cup water
¼ teaspoon rosewater (optional)
Whipped cream for serving

1. Combine the cranberries, sugar, and jelly in a small saucepan. Cook over low heat for 10 minutes. Set aside to cool.

2. Stir the softened gelatin and the rosewater, if using, into the cranberry mixture. Place the saucepan in the refrigerator. Chill for approximately 30 minutes.

3. When the cranberry filling is thoroughly chilled, pour it into the prepared crust. Refrigerate until serving.

4. To serve: Remove the sides of the springform pan and set the base on a cakestand. Serve with whipped cream.

RECIPE INDEX

RESOURCES

ARCHITECTURE

Camilla Mathlein
Millerton, New York 12546
917.453.8489
studiocm@mac.com
Space designer

Christine Krause Design Studio, Inc.
860.319.1900
christinekrausedesign.com
Landscape designer

Churchill Building Company, LLC
332 Main Street
Lakeville, Connecticut 06039
860.596.4063
churchillbuildingcompany.com
Builder

Jamie Purinton
518.329.2337
jamiepurinton.com
Landscape architect; focus on sustainable
plantings

Rafe Churchill
91 Main Street
Sharon, Connecticut 06069
860.364.2288
info@rafechurchill.com
Architect

MARKETS: FOOD AND PRODUCE

HUDSON VALLEY

Note: Many farm markets have irregular hours
or are only open in the summer season; it's
always best to call ahead.

Adams Fairacre Farms
1560 Ulster Avenue
Lake Katrine, New York 12449 (Kingston)
845.336.6300
(also in Poughkeepsie, Wappinger, and
Newburgh)
adamsfarms.com
Wide selection of produce, meats, fish, and
specialty foods; also flowers and plant nursery

Applestone Meat Company
4737 Route 209
Accord, New York 12404
845.626.4444
Locally raised hormone-free meat

Black Sheep Hill Farm
1891 County Route 83
Pine Plains, New York 12567
518.771.3067
blacksheephill.com
Heritage breed pigs and sheep, vegetables,
yarn, cage-free eggs

Chaseholm Farm:
    Amazing Real Live Food Co.
124 Chase Road
Pine Plains, New York 12567
518.398.0368
chaseholmfarm.com
Artisanal cheeses and other products
from a family farm

Davenport Farms
3411 Route 209
Stone Ridge, New York 12484
845.687.0051
davenportfarms.com
Farm stand featuring locally sourced
vegetables, meats, plants, flowers, and some
prepared foods

Fleishers Butcher Shop
307 Wall Street
Kingston, New York 12401
845.338.6666
fleishers.com
Specialty butcher shop featuring
farm-raised meats

Green Acres Farm
226 Route 82
Hudson, New York 12534
518.851.7460
greenacreshudson.com
Farm stand featuring vegetables and
homemade pies and preserves

Hathaway Young Specialty Foods
56 South Center Street
Millerton, New York 12546
860.596.0555
hathawayyoung.com
Bakery and café

Herondale Farm
90 Wiltsie Bridge Road
Ancramdale, New York 12503
518.329.3769
herondalefarm.com
Grass-fed beef, lamb, and
pasture-raised pork; charcuterie

High Falls Food Co-op
1398 Route 213
High Falls, New York 12440
845.687.7262
highfallsfoodcoop.com
Healthy, sustainable local food

Montgomery Place Orchards
8 Davis Way
Red Hook, New York 12504
845.758.6338
mporchards.com
Historic farm market featuring heirloom
fruits and vegetables

Pecks Food Market
2991 East Church Street
Pine Plains, New York 12567
518.398.6622
pecksmarket.shoptocook.com
All-purpose grocery with local produce

Pigasso Farms
500 Farm Road
Copake, New York 12516
518.929.3252
pigassofarms.com
Pasture-raised meats and eggs;
farm-cured charcuterie

Rock Steady Farm & Flowers
41 Kaye Road
Millerton, New York 12546
917.864.6198
info@rocksteadyfarm.com
Organically grown vegetables and flowers

Sky Acres Farm Market
481 County Route 7
Pine Plains, NY 12567
518.398.6015
skyacresangus.com
Pasture-raised meat and eggs

Sol Flower Farm
5744 Route 22
Millerton, New York 12546
518.592.1360
solflowerfarm@gmail.com
Farm stand featuring flowers, vegetables,
and seedlings

Thompson-Finch Farm
750 Wiltsie Bridge Road
Ancram, New York 12502
518.329.7578
thompsonfinch.com
Pick-your-own organic fruit

Westwind Orchard
215 Lower Whitfield Road
Accord, New York 12404
845.626.0659
Pick-your-own organic fruit

Willow Brook Farms
196 Old Post Road #4
Millerton, New York 12546
518.789.3289
Farm-raised meat, eggs, and vegetables

NEW ENGLAND

A Wee Bit Farm
Orland, Maine 04472
207.469.3319
aweebitfarm.com
Natural and farm-raised lamb and beef

Bizalion's Fine Food
684 Main Street, #3
Great Barrington, Massachusetts 01230
413.644.9988
bizalions.com
Specialty foods, including cheeses,
olive oils, wines, etc.

Browne Trading Market
262 Commercial Street
Portland, Maine 04101
207.775.7560
brownetrading.com
Gourmet market specializing in seafood

Dorolenna Farm
184 Berry Road
Center Montville, Maine 04941
207.322.6382
Family farm featuring organic
vegetables and fruit

Fine Line Farm
97 West Appleton Road
Searsmont, Maine 04973
207.589.6996
finelinefarm.wordpress.com
Family farm featuring organic
vegetables and eggs

Guido's Fresh Marketplace
760 Main Street
Great Barrington, Massachusetts 01230
413.528.4913
guidosfreshmarketplace.com
Full-service grocery featuring imported and
local cheeses, meats, fish, produce, prepared
foods, and gourmet items

LaBonne's Market
22 Academy Street
Salisbury, Connecticut 06068
860.435.2559
labonnes.com
Upscale grocery featuring fine imported
cheeses, specialty items, and prime meats

Morning Glory Natural Foods
60 Maine Street
Brunswick, Maine 04011
207.729.0546
moglonf.com
Local, natural, and organic foods

Morrill Century Farm
133 North Main Street
Morrill, Maine 04952
207.342.2496
morrillcenturyfarm.com
Fresh local produce, sustainably grown

Rising Tide Community Market
323 Main Street
Damariscotta, Maine 04543
207.563.5556
customercare@risingtide.coop
Organic local, farm-raised products

Villageside Farm
122 Belfast Road
P.O. Box 32
Freedom, Maine 04941
207.382.6300
villagesidefarm.com
Organic vegetables, flowers, and seedlings

PRODUCTS

HUDSON VALLEY, NEW ENGLAND,
NEW YORK CITY, AND ELSEWHERE

Berkshire Mountain Distillers
356 South Main Street
Sheffield, Massachusetts 01257
413.229.0219
berkshiremountaindistillers.com
Handcrafted artisanal spirits

Damascus Bakery
56 Gold Street
Brooklyn, New York 11201
718.625.7070
Artisanal flatbreads

Hillrock Estate Distillery
408 Pooles Hill Road
Ancram, New York 12502
518.329.1023
info@hillrockdistillery.com
Handcrafted spirits

The Hudson Standard
Hudson, New York 12534
518.755.4208
thehudsonstandard.com
Small batch bitters and syrups

In Pursuit of Tea
33 Brook Road
Cornwall Bridge, Connecticut 06754
860.248.3020
Fine teas from around the world

Jacüterie
Ancramdale, New York 12503
jacuterie.com
Handcrafted charcuterie

Jan's Farmhouse Crisps
112 South Main Street #227
Stowe, Vermont 05672
802.371.9712
Award-winning artisanal crackers

Kramer Knives
360.455.4357
info@kramerknives.com
Handcrafted collectible knives

Lost Ruby Farm
458 Winchester Road,
Norfolk, Connecticut 06058
860.542.5806
Locally made cheeses

Millbrook Vineyards & Winery
26 Wing Road
Millbrook, New York 12545
845.677.8383
millbrookwine.com
Established winery open for
occasional tours and tastings

Nuts.com
800.558.6887
nuts.com
Premium bulk nuts and dried fruit

Shelter Designs Yurts
101 North Johnson Street
Missoula, Montana 59801
406.721.9878
shelterdesigns.net
Montana-made yurts

Taartwork Pies
Brooklyn, New York
Taartworkpies.com
Adorable custom-made pies and tarts

WHERE TO EAT

HUDSON VALLEY, NEW ENGLAND,
AND NEW YORK CITY

Back in the Kitchen
3312 Route 343
Amenia, New York 12501
845.789.1444
Bakery and café

Berkshire Mountain Bakery
367 Park Street (Route 183)
Housatonic, Massachusetts 01236
413.274.1313
berkshiremountainbakery.com
Artisanal bakery and café

Bonfiglio & Bread
748 Warren Street
Hudson, New York 12534
518.822.0277
Bakery specializing in handmade
hearth breads and café

Chase's Daily
96 Main Street
Belfast, Maine 04915
207.338.0555
Vegetarian and vegan restaurant

The Farmer's Wife
3 County Route 8
Ancramdale, New York 12503
518.329.5431
thefarmerswife.biz
Breakfast and lunch; catering

Harney & Sons Tearoom
13 Main Street
Millerton, New York 12546
518.789.2121
433 Broome Street
New York, New York 10013
212.933.4853
Harney.com
Tearoom with fine teas from around the world

The Lost Kitchen
22 Mill Street
Freedom, Maine 04941
207.382.3333
Exceptional food with fresh, local ingredients

Manna Dew Café
54 Main Street
Millerton, New York 12546
518.789.3570
Farm-to-table fare

Mercato
61 East Market Street
Red Hook, New York 12571
845.758.5879
mercatoredhook.com
Italian artisanal fare

The Old Mill
53 Main Street
Route 23
South Egremont, Massachusetts 01258
413.528.1421
oldmillberkshires.com
Seasonal contemporary New England cuisine

Prairie Whale
178 Main Street
Great Barrington, Massachusetts 01230
413.528.5050
Rustic fresh food from local farms

Serevan
6 Autumn Lane
Amenia, New York 12501
845.373.9800
serevan.com
Seasonally inspired Middle Eastern and
Mediterranean food

Stissing House
7801 South Main Street
Pine Plains, New York 12567
518.398.8800
stissinghouse.com
Historic inn with classic French cuisine

The White Hart
15 Undermountain Road
Salisbury, Connecticut 06068
860.435.0030
whitehartinn.com
Restaurant and inn. Seasonal menu sourced by
nearby farms

WHERE TO SHOP

HUDSON VALLEY, NEW ENGLAND,
AND NEW YORK CITY

Finch
555 Warren Street
Hudson, New York 12534
518.828.3430
finchhudson.com
Vintage and modern goods for the home

Fishs Eddy
889 Broadway (at 19th Street)
New York, New York 10003
212.420.9020
fishseddy.com
Dishes, glassware, and so much more

Hammertown Barn
3201 Route 199
Pine Plains, New York
518.398.7075
Montgomery Row
Rhinebeck, New York 12572
845.876.1450
15 Bridge Street
Great Barrington, Massachusetts 01230
412.528.7766
Furnishings, antiques, and accessories
for your country home, and
interior and design services

Hunter Bee
21 Main Street
Millerton, New York 12546
518.789.2127
hunterbee.com
Country antiques and midcentury and
industrial finds

The Marston House
101 Main Street
(Route 1 at Middle Street)
P.O. Box 517
Wiscasset, Maine 04578
207.882.6010
marstonhouse.com
Antiques, architecture, and design; also a b&b

Michael Trapp
7 River Road
West Cornwall, Connecticut 06796
860.672.6098
michaeltrapp.com
Antiques, architectural fragments, and
interior and garden design services

Millerton Antiques Center
25 Main Street
Millerton, New York 12546
518.789.6004
millertonantiquescenter.com
Thirty-six antiques dealers

York Antiques Gallery
746 U.S. Route 1
York, Maine 03909
207.363.5002
yorkantiques.com
High-quality multi-dealer shop

ACKNOWLEDGMENTS

Entertaining is a group effort, as is book writing. We are so grateful to the families who allowed us into their inspiring country homes so we could study and record their entertaining styles: Drew Evans; Michael Hofemann and Andrew Arrick; Michael Trapp; Julia Turshen and Grace Bonney; Virginia Smith and Patrick Robinson; Dana and Jamey Simpson; Dana Cowin and Barclay Palmer; Brooke Lehman and Gregg Osofsky; Erin French; and Sharon and Paul Mrozinski. Special thanks to Serge Madikians of Serevan, and to Nicole LoBue of Kite's Nest. Many other friends contributed recipes and ideas to this book; thank you for your generous input. Thanks also are due to the farmers and artisans who produced the ingredients for these feasts. There is a genuine revolution going on in the world today in the way we grow and cook our food, and the small villages of the Hudson Valley and New England are at the forefront of this movement.

We have been incredibly fortunate in our talented team, the same small group that worked with us on our previous book, *Love Where You Live*. Warm thank-yous to Farley Chase, our literary agent; to stylist Wanda Furman, photographer John Gruen, book designer Doug Turshen, and to Sandy Gilbert Freidus, our wonderful editor at Rizzoli. Thanks also to Lynn Karlin, who contributed some of the photographs in this book, and Deborah Weiss Geline, our meticulous copyeditor.

We've truly become a family, and the spirit you see in these pages comes from the honor and respect we have for each other, and for the people who opened up their homes and hearts to us.

—Joan Osofsky and Abby Adams

Julia Turshen and Grace Bonney's collection of Delftware and blue transferware plates brightens a corner of the kitchen.

First published in the United States of America in 2017
by Rizzoli International Publications, Inc.
300 Park Avenue South
New York, New York 10010
www.rizzoliusa.com

Printed in China
ISBN 13: 978-0-8478-5883-5
Library of Congress Cataloging-in-Publication Data: 2016958247

Project Editor: Sandra Gilbert
Editorial Assistance provided by Hilary Ney, Deborah Weiss Geline, Deri Reed, and Tricia Levi
Production Manager: Susan Lynch
Art Direction: Doug Turshen with Steve Turner

Cocktails on the Terrace: Thank you to the companies and people who helped make the
"LIVE eat LOCAL"-themed party possible, many of which are listed in the Resources. We would also like
to extend our thanks to Annie Quigley for her charming poster and label design.

FRONT ENDPAPER: A pair of his-and-her swings beckons under a massive old tree outside Dana Cowin and Barclay Palmer's
Hudson Valley weekend retreat. BACK ENDPAPER: Rosé and hors d'oeuvres in the garden—a perfect beginning for a summer party.
Dana and Jamey Simpson's home is set in a forty-acre clearing surrounded by forests and the foothills of the Berkshires.